# Gifted

## 2005 Poetry Collection

Published by
The America Library of Poetry
P.O. Box 978
Houlton, ME 04730
Website: www.libraryofpoetry.com
Email: generalinquiries@libraryofpoetry.com

Printed in the United States of America

THE AMERICA
LIBRARY OF POETRY

ISBN 0-9773662-0-0

# Contents

From the American Literacy Council ............................ 4

Foreword .................................................................. 5

About the Editor's Choice Award............................... 6

Spirit of Education Award .......................................... 7

## Poetry by Division

Division I
Grades 4-5 ............................................................. 9

Division II
Grades 6-7 ............................................................ 77

Division III
Grades 8-9 .......................................................... 137

Division IV
Grades 10-12........................................................ 195

Index of Authors.................................................... 218

Gifted Ordering Information.................................... 223

Poetry On the Web Information ............................224

# From the American Literacy Council

What do the American Literacy Council
and the America Library of Poetry have in common?
We're all in it for love of the poetry.
By poetry I mean compositions designed to convey a vivid sense of experience.
That's the heart of poetry, and it's also the heart of writing:
from kids gleefully writing on walls with crayons
to adults dutifully writing cover letters on laptops—
we're all trying to convey a vivid sense of experience.
We all want to be understood and appreciated.

The America Library of Poetry understood and appreciated this longing
in eliciting a wide array of compositions via its poetry contest.
We are delighted to work with them again
by featuring one of their award-winning poems in our Sound-Write software,
where the poem (by its example) will encourage users of all ages
to convey a vivid sense of experience.

For a free demo of our writing software
with immediate audio-visual feedback,
visit our website at www.americanliteracy.com/software.htm
(for a quick download), call us at (800)781-9985, or
email us at fyi@americanliteracy.com

Joe Little
Managing Director
American Literacy Council

# Foreword

There are two kinds of writers in the world.
There are those who write from experience, and those who write from imagination.
The experienced, offer words that are a reflection of their lives.
The triumphs they have enjoyed, the heartaches they have endured;
all the things that have made them who they are,
they graciously share with us, as a way of sharing themselves,
and in doing so, give us, as readers, someone to whom we may relate,
as well as fresh new perspectives
on what may be our common circumstances in life.
From the imaginative, come all the wonderful things we have yet to experience;
from sights unseen, to sounds unheard.
They encourage us to explore the limitless possibilities of our dreams and fantasies,
and aid us in escaping, if only temporarily,
the confines of reality and the rules of society.
To each, we owe a debt of gratitude;
and rightfully so, as each provides a service of equal importance.
Yet, without the other, neither can be truly beneficial.
For instance, one may succeed in accumulating a lifetime of experience,
only to consider it all to have been predictable and unfulfilling,
if denied the chance to chase a dream or two along the way.
Just as those whose imaginations run away with them, never to return,
may find, that without solid footing in the real world, life in fantasyland is empty.
As you now embark, dear reader,
upon your journey through these words to remember,
you are about to be treated to both heartfelt tales of experience,
and captivating adventures of imagination.
It is our pleasure to present them for your enjoyment.
To our many authors,
who so proudly represent the two kinds of writers in the world,
we dedicate this book, and offer our sincere thanks;
for now, possibly more than ever,
the world needs you both.

*Paul Wilson Charles*

Editor

# Editor's Choice Award

The Editor's Choice Award is presented to the author
who, more than any other, in our opinion,
demonstrates not only the solid fundamentals of correct writing form,
word usage, grammar, and punctuation,
but also, the ability to illicit an emotional response
or provide a thought provoking body of work
in a manner which is both clear and concise.

You will find "Father" by Sara Marie Johnson
on page 217 of "Gifted".

# Spirit of Education
## For Outstanding Participation

# 2005

# Almond Tree
# Middle School
# Delano, California

Presented to participating students and faculty
in recognition of your commitment to literary excellence.

# Division I

# Grades 4-5

# Heaven
### by Lauren A. Bennett

Kids play with newfound friends
Finding love that never ends
People laughing, jumping about
They're all having fun, no doubt
Even though we're not with them right now
They're still resting in our hearts somehow
We know that God took them for a reason
They are the ones that make the colors of the seasons
I love them, but their flesh is done
So now they are my sun


# Cupid
### by Timea Sipos

Diving, lurking
Searching for love
Swishing, slashing
Bow and arrow
Work is done


# Summer Days
### by Allison Eacrett

Looking through the window
Sun in my eyes
It's a beautiful day
Wish I was playing outside
Fun in the pool
Splashing away
Playing games with my friends
Hoping the fun never ends


# You Are Gone, But I Will See You
### by Rainie Borges

Grandpa, Grandpa
All the memories I have of you will always be there
But you won't
We had good times and will have more
When I see you in Heaven, forever more

## Untitled
### by Katherine Hall

Singing is my passion
It is me, not you; it is my dream!
It is my vocals; it is almost like my IQ
When I sing, I think of the beautiful flowers in the blue clear air
I think of friends and family, just anything beyond compare
I also think of how my dad gave my mom that big rock on her finger
Which, she still has today
This is all my passion in singing
So, do you understand? Okay! But, I'm not yet, okay?
You see, there is still more passion in me
When I think of my grandma and granddad and how they tell the history of me
Or when my little cousin just learned to say her name, "Me! Me!"
Well, that is all my passion from now to the end
But now my dream story has just began


## Scary Mountain
### by Chad Bolotin

It is the end of fall; I am going hiking
The snow beating against my face
The water dripping down my throat
It is getting late in the afternoon
The breeze making me freeze; freeze like an ice cube
My cheeks are turning pink
The higher I go the more tired I get
The sun is going down, it is getting dark
I stop, look around, nothing's there
I hear a big roar
I hear it again, talking to myself, worrying
"Who's there?" I whispered
It got dark I should go home
Something is surrounding me
I pull my flashlight out; I see these eyes staring at me
Then I shone my flashlight; it was gone

# Farms
### by Lauren Taylor Harding

Farms have ponds
Farms have hills
Grassy grounds
All around
Many trees
A couple turkeys
Cows, sheep, guinea hens
Dogs, cats, horses
And one little fox
The chickens and the deer
Grew up on the hills
They too love
A farm called
Echo Hill!

# My Monkey
### by Daniel Johnson

My big brown monkey
Is really very funky
He is very fuzzy
And likes to be quite buzzy
My monkey eats bananas by the pound
And throws his peelings on the ground
Yes, you might say my monkey is funky

# Orphan Girl
### by Madeleine Blackman

Scared of commitment because of the aching of a recent death
She just lives life, thinking of him
Of what he would say, what he would think, what he would do
The name rings through her head, depressing her
Thinking of her past foster parents that she ran away from
His face comes to mind, every wrinkle, every crease
Abandoned at birth, she always wished for a family
Now she has one and it burns in her heart that he's not in it

# The Stars
### by Gabriella Cobar

The night is very bright
With the stars hangin' from the sky
My grandmother died
This very night
Everybody was heartbroken
And this was the token
To watching the stars
Shooting stars, bright stars
If you look closely
You might see Mars
Constellations
Motivations
A lot of stars
But now I must lie down
So tomorrow I don't frown!

# My Darling Centipede
### by Peri Tur

Dear little centipede
With all your darling feet
I often wonder how it is we came to meet
You walking through the park
Me, my merry way
Never once thinking that we would meet one day
Now you are a father of many little tykes
And for Christmas we will buy them 100 peddle bikes
Now I sign with love so sincere and so true
So proud and so happy that I had married you

# Feelings
### by Peri Bilbo-Gildersleeve

Feelings are a good thing to me
They're cool, pretty, and can be free
It's a good feeling
Or a warm healing
It's good when I pray on my knee

## Killer Whales
### by Brandon Bolster

Killer whales are black and white
Although they're killers they do not fight
They swim all night and play all day
And when they work at Sea World they get a lofty pay
And if I might say they also eat seals all day
But they never stay
They love ice and are very nice indeed
And they swim at such great speed
But air is a need to this mammal indeed
They swim very fast
And have great body mass
Whales swim down canals
But they also make great pals


## Peter Pan
### by Jessica Fitzpatrick

Flying magically
Spreading fairy dust
Disney World
Wishing upon stars
Making children happy


## Spring
### by Catherine Regan

Winter, spring, summer, and fall
I'd like to tell you my favorite of all
Flowers bloom; the sun shines longer
I crave warm days and I feel I am stronger
Filled with promise and blooms
Gone are the days sitting inside rooms
Outside I can play sports and games
Along with learning new people's names
Swimming and playing with a friend
It gives memories till the end
Spring is the season that I like most
Gone are the dark days with the winter ghost

## Falcons In the Mountains
### by Robert S. Jenkins

Falcons in the mountains sailing in the sky through the clouds
Puff in, puff out
Wichew, wichew
In hopes of uncovering prey on the top of his own mountain
The glimmering eyes in the morning sun
Perched on a tree limb waiting for a rabbit
To pass by his tree at the top of the mountain
On that very night it squatted on the same limb mending his silky-fluffy feathers
Falcons in the mountains are resting through the night

## Flower
### by Melinda Gudelia Guzman

Flower
Beautiful, fluffy
Swift back and forth, grow, bloom
I feel calm
Tiny plant

## Diamante For Alisa
### by Alisa Word

Circle
Round, sideless
Bouncing, shining, glistening
Dot, earring, food, word
Playing, sleeping, eating
Short, efficient
Self

## Plains
### by Brandon J. Rodriguez

Plain plains, why?
Bison gone
Rattlers moved out and left
Cacti dried out and shriveled to dust
Like a graveyard at night
Plain, like a desert plain

# The Crazy New York Streets
## by Jocelyn Swenson

Taxis honking, cars screeching, people rushing by
The whoosh of the subway
Nightclubs, Broadway plays, people running to catch taxis
Street dancers, lost people asking for directions
Restaurant signs, bright lights
The crazy New York streets, towering skyscrapers
Street vendors, people riding bikes
People hurrying, street musicians
The hiss of tour buses
Golden statues
The crazy New York streets


# The Boy I Want To Meet
## by Kelly Martin

The song I want to sing is about a boy I want to meet
I'm not sure what he'd be like, but I know he'd be nice
I don't know how tall or how small
I'm not sure of his hair or what he likes to wear
I don't know what he sounds like or what sport he does
But I bet he's probably competitive
I hope that he's smart and has a great personality
But I don't know that's just reality
Well all of these questions are for another day
So for now it's so long until that day


# Fairy Tales
## by Cassie Gestl

Do you believe in fairy tales?
Do you believe that dreams can come true?
Well I do
I remember when I was a little girl and my mom used to tuck me in at night
And read me a fairy tale by moonlight!
What do you think when you hear fairy tales
I think knights, princess, and the passion in love
I think dreams, the unbelievable can happen
Some things don't go together in fairy tales
Sometimes it's unreal, I think about it when days go by
But I believe in fairy tales at night
I do, I do, I believe in fairy tales; do you!?

# Happiness
## by Stevie Schultz

So early, it's still almost dark out
I'm near the window with coffee
And the usual early morning stuff that passes for thought
When I see a girl and her friend walking up the road to deliver the newspaper
They are wearing caps and sweaters
And one girl has a bag over her shoulder
They are so happy
They aren't even saying anything
These girls


# I Wish
## by Stephanie Brewster

I wish I could go, run far away
Drift away just for one day
Leave this drama here to stay
To hear the seagulls and the ocean blue
Don't you want to go too?
I wish I could race across the field
And for no one I would have to yield


# Black
## by Christian Petri

Black is what I mostly wear
When I leave, people mostly stare
Black is all I have inside
Sometimes I just want to sit and cry
That is what I have to say
I will not die till the day
When I seem to sit and cry
Revealing how I feel inside
Thank you for this cool life
Soon I might have a wife
If I don't end this life

# Untitled
## by Tori Rhodes

A beautiful imagination is like a rose
Sitting under the sun and a beautiful sunset rushing over the sky
Imagination is the only thing that inspires you
It makes you fill with joy and love
Imagination can be fun when you are at the beach with the palm trees
And the beautiful water, with the sun reflecting off of it into a beautiful sight
Let your imagination grow into a bush of roses and thorns
You could need it one day for all of the wonderful signs of greatness

# My Pool
## by Laura Christine Casey

Summer is hot
But I'm not
Summer is cool to me
Because I have a pool, you see
A pool is fun
But what about the sun?
The sun is hot
But I'm not
Because I have a pool
To keep me cool!

# Detention
## by Jori Porterfield

Sitting in detention, it's so boring here
Something gets my attention; I'm getting bored to tears
Then I see a field with flowers on the trees
While sitting in that field there comes a nice cool breeze
Then it's not so nice, it turns dark and gray
I see a pair of mice, what happened to this day?
Along comes a snake, a poison one at that
I fight it away; it lands with a splat
I suddenly feel a shake; I start to fall down
With a fright I wake then I start to frown
If it was all a dream why did it feel so real?
I guess it just seems that's the way I feel

## Slithering Snakes
**by Lisa Wu**

A
Snake
Slithers and crawls
They run in their dreams
Fly in their dreams
And they
Slide and slip
In their reality


## Beauty of the Wilderness
**by Alice Sun**

The mild wind left a soft rustle behind the fresh, green trees
The wilderness is filled with busy, energetic, and buzzing bees
As the razor-sharp grass swayed
I stared up with my glistening eyes and laid
A beautiful bird merrily chirped by
As I was still lying in the clear, warm, midday sky
The rabbits hopping freely in the golden field
Protecting my fears like a polished silver shield
Sweet spring blossoms carried a whimsical scent
Making every little creature happy and content
There are so many little messages to send
In the nature's refreshing peppermint wind


## Prowl
**by Julia Beth Airey**

A flash of red, a tail tip white
The fox is on the prowl
From snow covered trees to stick bare shrubs
She darts to and fro across a pond, over a bridge
Wind howls relentlessly, no birds are chirping
The forest carries a scent of forbidden
Desperate for a rabbit call she presses on
Suddenly, jaws clamp around her paw, piercing the flesh
The fox bites the metal jaws, but to no avail
As the hours pass, cold settles in
And as the blood continues to flow, life does not
Humans are on the prowl

## Limerick
### by Marissa K. Rowlett

There once was a dog named Bear
Who shed and shed his hair
He was big and tall
Not short or small
And once almost sat in a chair!

## My Brother
### by Broderick Rohan States

My brother is a real pain
And sometimes drives me insane
And then I remember that fact
That we will always love each other

## Springtime
### by Rachel Keen

Springtime, when the robins twitter
You hear the children laughing
The air has changed to sweet from bitter
You can't believe it's happening
"School's almost out!" the children scream
Mom's spring-cleaning
Dad's trying to make the lawn green
Everyone is beaming
Weather's getting warmer
Windows are open; fans are on
Summer's getting closer
Wanna race, you're on!
Critters creeping through the woods
Scurrying around gathering food
In a hole they hide their goods
A chat with them will lighten your mood
Springtime, when the robins twitter
You hear the children laughing
The air has changed to sweet from bitter
You can't believe it's happening

# My Sense Poem
### by Mason M. Unruh

Mad, mad is red
Mad smells like burnt hot dogs
Mad feels like a thorn bush
Mad tastes like rotten milk
Mad looks like war
Mad sounds like bombs going off behind you


# Tropical Island
### by Taylor Weisman

On an island after it rains
I see sugar canes
When I get there
The animals don't give a care
I walked by a bear
And he gives me a mean glare
I run for my life
Good thing I wasn't carrying a knife
Then I passed through a river
Then I gave a shiver
Good thing that bear can't swim


# Outside My Classroom Window
### by Kelsie Godfrey

Oh, how I wish I could see Mount Rushmore
Or at least have some kind of tour!
Even the waves of the sea would be pretty
Or even a store across the street that seems a bit witty
A store full of mice that smells like spice
Hey! I would even take a bucket full of ice
I would not even think twice
If I could just have a view
All I can see from my classroom window
Is the wall of our school!

## Monkeys At the Zoo
### by Shyanna Woods

Monkey see, monkey do
You'll see them at the zoo
Swinging high from tree to tree
Eating bananas just like me
Throwing yellow banana peels
After eating all their meals
Picking fleas off their heads
Getting tired, time for bed
Monkeys jumping up and down
Beating their tummies, just like a clown
That's what monkeys do
When you see them at the zoo

## I Hear
### by Torieana Alexis St.Pierre

I hear the bird scream like old violins
I hear a church pray and sing
I hear the tide come closer to the hot sand
I hear two or three cars racing down the road
I hear the wind blow straight through the leaves of a tree
I hear people playing and giggling
I hear all the different sounds of the world

## Happy Valentine's Day
### by Kayla Criswell

There's a lot to say
Let's start with Happy Valentine's Day
Thanks for keeping us from harm
You are my lucky charm
You are the entire rave
For all the acts you do so brave
I hope you like this card
Because it was so hard
Thanks for all you do
And know that someone loves you

# Life Is Precious
## by Domonique Campbell

Life is like a diamond; life is like gold
I wish there wasn't a way to get old
Life is so sacred; life is so free
God I thank you for helping me to believe
God I thank you for helping me to see
Life is for you to enjoy; doesn't matter if you are a girl or boy
Don't despise your life; you need to come open your eyes
Life is like the sun strong and bright
Your eyes are light that gives you sight
Don't be twenty-five, dead or hurt for money
Get a job so you can live, get married, and be called honey
"Do right," is what God said
He gave his only Son for us, who lives but yet was dead
So I thank you Savior for my life; I will love Him for life


# Falcon
## by Kayla-Marie Arenas

Fly falcon
Fly, high, soar
Beautiful bird
Fast, slick
No limits, fly


# Bailey
## by Cameron Bugbee

His name is Bailey
People say he's daily
He is brown with a big fat frown
He went to the park to find a dog
There was a fire in the fog
So he went to the town to the station
And they all were on vacation
He went to a friend, "bark bark"
They followed him, then put out the fire
After they took a break and started to rake
The day ended just as well
So good night

# Untitled
## by Miranda Cummings

My mother, my father
My grandparents, too
Cherish and love me
All the way through
They hug and they kiss
Everyone they love
My family will always
Always be loved!

# Animals
## by Lauren Stark

A tiny, fluffy hamster
Can be quite a little clamster
A sweet, beautiful horse
Wouldn't even go a course
A big, smart cat
Would have a dunce hat
A silly, nutty dog
Would be smarter than a hog
A small, yellow mockingbird
Wouldn't say a word
The animals would do all these
So if you would, pretty please
Don't kill animals
Especially the ones on Danimals

# What I Want For a Pet
## by Amanda Veronica Rios

What I want for a pet
Well, what do you want for a pet?
Well, what I want for a pet is a dog
Maybe other kids like hamsters, cats, dogs, parrot snakes, fish
And lots of other animals, but I like dogs
Mostly any kind of dog or any kind of animal, but a dog is my favorite
But any person can like any kind of animal
And no one can stop you from liking that one animal

## Middle of the Forest
### by Josh Fortier

The middle of the forest
You're lost, you don't know where you are
It feels like you'll never find light, food, or life again
No one around to call for help
No houses, no phones, no anything
You're all alone
Sounds of wolves, bears, and all other animals
Only your footsteps to follow back home
You can't see light
You can smell the oak trees
You taste your mouth craving for food
At night you see nothing ... nothing at all


## Trees
### by Josh Harrington

Trees are some of the only definite things in life
Standing there day after day
Seeming to die in the winter and then being reborn
As soon as spring's gentle warmth comes
Trees are timeless, ageless portals to the past
Silent witnesses to all that happens
The wisest of all living things
Trees share their home with all animals
Trees are larger and more powerful than all of us
Humans cannot even fathom the wisdom of trees
Trees defy the superiority of humans
Holding the secrets of the past
Trees have vast memories of everything they witness
Trees came before humans and will continue after our species is wiped out


## A Friend
### by Monika Grant

A friend is a gift of caring and kindness
A friend can fly away if you don't hold tight like a balloon
Every friend is different like a kitten
One may have spots, the other have stripes
Friends can be a cat, a dog or a person
It does not matter the color type or where they're from
Because a friend will always be there for you

# A Day At the Beach
### by Keyonna Murphy

Oh, today I went to the beach
I could not believe the wonderful sandy beach
And right there in front of me, in the sand
Was a delicious pink peach
Suddenly, there was a loud sound of thunder
Which was scary and I really wondered
Would the storm go away until another day?
If the storm would, then I could make a sand castle really big
I felt a big bump in the sand and began to dig
I found in the sand a rock with a big hump
What a wonderful castle it would make for me
To end my day at the beach


# Friends
### by Taylor C. Penndorf

Friends are people you can trust, people that don't talk behind your back
Friends know when you are happy or sad
Friends are people who you can hang out with any time
You know when you get hurt, friends are always by your side
When you have a problem, you know you can tell your friends
With great friends like you guys, life is complete for me
I hope we always stay together; true friends are forever
They never say goodbye!


# Where Is My Family?
### by Leah Victoria Myrtil

Where is my family?
Are they here?
Are they there?
I do not see them anywhere
I look up and I look down
I could not hear a sound
Everywhere I walk
I do not hear a sound
I went downstairs and then I heard
"One, two, three! Surprise! Surprise!"
They are here!

# Tigers
### by Savanah Pruitt

Tigers
Bodies with black
And orange, they make me think
Of Halloween, what about you?
Tigers

# 9 x 9 = 81
### by Allison Kurpiel

Nine times nine equals eighty-one
To help us remember we'll have some fun
Katie wanted nine cookies
So she went to Mr. Hookies
And found out that they each cost a dime
And boy did they taste fine!

# All Alone
### by Katryna Kusmirek

All alone
Desperately I moan
Nothing to see
No one to be
Neglected
Affected
By one who doesn't care
It's just not fair
To be alone
And think that no one cares

# Having Fun
### by Elliott Mann

I like to play outside and climb on top of my house; it is fun
I like to boss around my little brother and act like I knock him down in the sun
I love to climb my tree
When I do it, I feel so free
I like to go outside
And when I do it, I like to hide

# Purple
## by Alexandra Sanford

Purple is grapes when you squish them in your mouth
Purple is my birthstone, the amethyst when I was born in the South
Purple is the steam when you just get out of the shower
Purple is a special lavender flower
Purple is the name of our state bird
Purple is an echo that you just heard
Purple is unique, courageous, and calm
Purple is my friend, Darien, and purple is dawn
Purple is a bath bead and a candle light
Purple is cool, happy, and bright
Purple is also the sister of blue
Maybe purple can be your favorite color too

# The Butterfly
## by Phoebe Heins

A butterfly is a bud blooming in spring
It is incense billowing up from the box that beholds it
A butterfly is a colorful gift from the clouds
It is an angel sitting senseless on a fragile leaf
A butterfly is as graceful as a star in the blackest night
It is a feather floating in the wind
A butterfly is as quick and sly as a skittish fox
It flees from everyone who tries to stroke its wings

# Lost In Literature
## by Rachael Hannah Zemanek

Help me! I'm lost in literature!
How this happened is totally obscure
But still, I'm lost in literature
I'm killed by a dragon, eaten by a whale
Tossed by the ocean's whipping gale
On the bus, on a train
Under an umbrella stuck in the rain
To have an adventure, but don't know where to look?
Open the pages of a really good book

## Michael Phelps
### by Adam Ekengren

Michael Phelps won the gold
He is not very old
Swimming laps in a pool
Year after year made Phelps cool

## Justin
### by Hannah King

My mean cousin makes me mad
I could just wring his neck
He makes me mad everyday
Justin

## Tanner
### by Sydney Rathjen

Tanner was a good friend
Till the very end
And it was very sad
But I was a little glad
I know that he is happy
Sleeping in the stars
And playing with new friends
But still, I sometimes wish
Our friendship wouldn't end

## Untitled
### by Jennifer Lynn Byrne

The trees are as green as a green jellybean
The sunset is red like the color of your bed
The sky is blue just like it's new
The clouds are white like a very bright light

# Orange
### by Taylor Vogt

Orange is the warmness of the sun
Orange is fire burning hot in the cold night
Orange is fierce during a fight
Orange is brave and stronger than anything
Orange is leaves falling down during the autumn season
Orange is Doritos waiting in a bag to be eaten
Orange is orange juice that you drink when you are eating breakfast
Orange is coolness during a windy summer day
Orange is the color that rocks this world


# Untitled
### by Amber Patrick

There once was a hen
Who lived in the den
She laid an egg
And bit her leg
Cried and cried till ten


# Fishing Down the Vineyard
### by J.R. Zizza, Jr.

My dad, wearing a tee shirt with a black dog, took me fishing
We used live, squirmy eels for bait to catch a striped bass
When we dropped the eel in the water for two seconds
We felt a tug and the rod was bent
It felt as if the rod was going to shatter in two pieces
Suddenly the rod came back up; the line was broken
The fish must have swallowed the hook
My dad hooked another slippery eel on the hook
The same striped bass gulped the eel down, almost broke the line
But this time my dad used the gath, a big pole with a hook on the end
As my dad lifted the gath, I noticed that the fish was almost sliced in half
We dropped the fish on the dock; it was still wiggling
My uncle measured it by counting his huge shoes against the fish
We found out that the striped bass was more than three feet long
It was the biggest fish that I ever caught, the first striped bass I ever caught
One hour later my dad, uncle and cousins ate a delicious meal of striped bass
Eating everything off their plate, but I didn't eat anything, because I don't like fish

# As I Watch Those Flowers Bloom
## by Brynn Foley

As I watch those flowers bloom
They sprout and I assume
That one day they will turn into beautiful flowers
So that I can see them from the highest towers
As I sit and watch what is going on
I want to stay and watch until dawn
All around I see the green, green grass
The flowers turn more beautiful even as I pass
Then the night shade has to come
And I go inside still chewing on my gum
I tuck myself into bed
"Good night, little girl," my mom said


# Lily
## by Rebecca Gilligan

There once was a girl named Lily
Who was always being so silly
She appears in my dreams
Yells out and screams
And that's the story of Lily


# The Snow Is Falling
## by Hannah-Grace McKenzie

The snow is falling, falling down
The snow is falling to the ground
The snow is falling, falling down
It looks like crystals on the ground
The snow is falling, falling down
It is covering my town
The snow is falling, falling down
Quietly, quietly, without a sound
The snow is falling from above
Like sparkles in the night and through my window
I can see the snow falling
Falling, waiting for me

# Dreams
## by Ilena Burnett

My dream is…
Cotton candy clouds up on the sky
Strangers always saying, "Hi"
No more cut knees and shots
No more cold weather; it's always hot
Every kid flies up in the sky
Floating ships are passing by
It's raining Skittles and bubble gum
Everywhere you go
No more parents saying, "No"
Hey, am I dreaming?


# Seasons
## by Michael Gaziano

Spring is here; the flowers have come
Spring is here and so is the sun
Summer is here; the grass is green
Summer is here as I swim in the stream
Fall is here; the leaves are colored
Fall is here; the birds have fluttered ... south
Winter is here; snowflakes are falling
Winter is here; we all are crawling ... in the snow
Throughout the year, seasons are here


# Guess Who?
## by Courtney Kossick

Stretching in the sunlight; yawning in the morning
Black coat glistening; tail so happily twitching
Yellow eyes peeking from her post, purring sounds from deep in her throat
He sits on the stone for the world to see, eating his peanuts so contently
Small and brown with a stripe down his back
When danger appears, to his den he goes back
Sitting on the tree silently; hooting to the moonlight
Hoot, hoot, flying in the night sky
Looking for mice, so high in the sky
Its night vision is so sharp
The bone he is chewing is almost gone, scratching his ears and wagging his tail
He barks at all danger that is near
Can you guess who these animals are?

## The Journey
### by Tess McCarthy

Leaves are falling through the sky
You can see them passing by
When they fall into the stream
Their journey starts, another dream

## Family Dinner
### by Tommy Moran

Family dinner is such a blast
We've had so many in the past
The dinner this time, it's our turn to make
We cook and we stir, and sometimes we bake
Piece by piece we chip away
By dinnertime we say, "Hurray!"
From experience we all know
That cooking light is the way to go
The family comes; it's such a treat
We all get together and sit down to eat
We chat and we laugh and sometimes we play
It's really a great way to end the day
The dishes are cleaned and it's time to go
But there's one more thing I want you to know
These dinners are special, my family's just right
When we all come together and share a great night

## Fog
### by Abigail Luchs

It's roaming through the valley
It's climbing up the hills
It's creeping through the alleys
It's giving me the chills
It's rolling towards our house
It's coming much too soon
It's as quiet as a mouse
It's covering up the moon

# Sunset
## by Madeline Russo

Yellow, pink, purple, turquoise, blue
Paint a picture in the sky
Brightening up the night with their wondrous light
Peaceful, full of color and excitement
Which is why people really like it
Happy sunset puts you in a trance
Oblivious to everything else around you
But the bright colors making your mind wander

# The Weird Thing I Saw
## by Takashi Nash

I saw something very weird
A very tall baby with a very big beard
And it wasn't fake
I checked to be awake
Maybe I should get a beard

# Untitled
## by Kimberly Hutner

There once was a boy named Chad
Who went grocery shopping with his dad
He looked in the bag
And started to brag
Because all he saw was a petite little lad

# Fire
## by Colin Williams

Fire, mysterious yet destructive, blazing in all its colors
It can be a tool and a weapon
Its glorious colors red, orange, yellow and blue
Going burning, flaming, destroying
It provides light to us, it can also burn down your home
Remember if you play with fire you'll get burned
Fire, traveling anywhere; no boundaries, no limits
No one commands fire
It burns wood, melts metal, and takes buildings to their knees
Leaves nothing but ash behind, no controls, fire

## Camping
### by Danielle Orr

Sleeping outside in a tent is fun
Even though wolves howl when there is no sun
Roasting marshmallows by the fire
Is better than calling someone sire
Eating hot dogs makes me hurl
Even though I am a girl
Fishing is fun
Especially in the sun
That's why I love camping!

## Florida
### by Shannon Vargas

I can hear the water splashing
And I see the light blue water
Then I touch the warm sand
Smell the ocean smell
And taste the salty water

## Japan
### by Daja Taylor

I want to go to Tokyo
Some people say it's weird
But I just reply, "So"
I plan to live there someday
Going to Tokyo is one of my many dreams
I wish to play in the big arcade
I'd bet Japan's more beautiful than it seems
Going there is my biggest dream and it will not fade
Tokyo is the best
I don't care what they say
Forget about the rest
I will live there someday

# Waterfall
## by Kaitlyn Flynn

Rivulets of water tumble into very cold puddles
Water clattering over the rocks in Canada
The wind blowing kids' hair, who are standing above the falls
Leaves plunge like little sailboats
Sun glancing at the big cascade through the trees
Trees' reflections shimmy on the water
Girls and boys, men and women
Perch at the picnic tables and munch on their hot dogs and cheeseburgers
The sun sets behind the falls

# The City Life
## by Casey Rowland

Hopscotch on streets
People to meet
This is life in the city
Horns are honkin'
People are talkin'
This is life in the city
Taxis are rollin'
People are strollin'
This is life in the city
The city that's bright
The city of lights
This is the city life

# The Seasons
## by Grace Cole

Spring, summer, winter, and fall
What is the difference? I don't know at all
In all of the seasons I still get my teasins'
I play in the day, and at night there I lay
But as I get older, I begin to see
That they are all different, all different to me
In the summer I'm hot and in winter I'm not
In the spring I'm silly and in the fall I'm chilly
So every season as you may see, is different – at least to me

## My Friend ... Him
### by Lauren Caprile

My disaster happened seven years ago
I was winning a medal in gymnastics – look at me go
The next day, I didn't see him
My best friend ever since
No one can replace him
Well, maybe one
But, anyway, he was big fun
I didn't know what happened
But, still he's just a friend named Him!

## Flowers
### by Dani Dame

Flowers bloom in the spring
Some look like they are kings
The Daisies are the best to me
Also maybe the bees
People plant them in the summer
The color of the rose could be a hummer
They are supposed to be in a garden
They are not supposed to harden
They are very pretty
Keep them away from your kitty

## If It Were All Up To Me
### by Paris Caldwell

If it were all up to me
The poor would have riches and the blind man would see
The hungry would eat, the weak will be strong
And the people who hated would all get along
The ones who were greedy will share
The unfriendly would care
The thirsty would drink, the deaf will hear
And sorrow and sadness would all disappear
The people in Hell would be kind enough to live in Heaven
That's how the world would be if it were all up to me
However, since it is not all up to me, I'll leave it to the pro of all living things
To make the world how I would want it!

## Love
### by Brandy Divine

Love, love is what I see
Love is everywhere you go
It's inside your heart, don't you know?
Love is a special thing
When you turn left or when you turn right
There is love everywhere
If you believe in love, it would believe in you

## See the Sea
### by Giovanni Korsko

If you want to see the sea
You need to be patient
In order to get to the sea
You need to have the key
The key to the sea
Is to be free

## SpongeBob and His Friends
### by Jenna Albulet

Patrick is pink, SpongeBob is yellow
This is a story about a few fellows
SpongeBob and Patrick are great pals
Gary, the snail, like a cat says meow
One evening, SpongeBob and Planktin go jellyfishing
They both have a song and it goes like this
F is for friends that do stuff together
U is for you and me
N is for anywhere anytime at all down
Here in the deep blue sea
Then Planktin says, "No! No! No! It's really
F is for fire that burns down the whole town
U is for uranium, bomi
N is for no survivors when you are all alone
F is for frolic through all the flowers
U is for ukulele
N is for nose picking, sharing gum, and sand liking
Here with my best buddy, ha ha ha ha ha
Ha ha ha ha ha ha ha ha!

# Dogs
### by Molly Boylan

Big, small, short, and tall
Some are fluffy like a ball
Some like to cuddle
Some like to play
Others have to have it their own way

# Friends
### by Brooke Pelletier

Friends are your buddies
They can always be your friends
Either black or white

# Libraries
### by Sophia Poulos

Libraries now look mainly the same
Exploding with pictures of celebrities of fame
Bursting with books with vivid colors
Full of scientists, astronauts, and baseball sluggers
Libraries are great for getting away
From baby brothers and sisters that run around all day
Libraries are quiet and very still
Which is great for research or homework drill
Librarians are generous about how they help me
With things I don't know or that I can't see
Or when I'm stuck on the website's home page
Pulling me out of a confused stage
Libraries may change very soon
With levitating science books of the stars and moon
Books will change in the next ten years
Filled with things that the past would surely fear
Computers, even though they're already advanced
In a few years, won't stand a chance
Against machines with opening and closing slots
Computers – acting like robots
Though books and computers change every day
Making a difference in a great way
Changes in them will be for the better
Books and computers will stay forever!

# Spring
### by Maia Tracy

In the spring
There is rain
In the spring
There is pain
When there is rain
It will rain
If you are not in pain

# Camping
### by Erisa Hoxhalli

Fire in the dark woods
Crackling loudly in stillness
Fresh scents everywhere

# Puppies
### by Katlin Repetti

Puppies
Sweet, cute
Barking, eating, playing
Loving, caring, perky, happy
Babies

# Bears
### by Casey Cirillo

There are Polar Bears, Panda Bears, and Grizzly Bears
Black Bears and Brown Bears, White Bears and Gray Bears
But my favorite type of bear is ... Teddy Bears!
So soft and cute, cuddly too
Brown, Black, White
Some are even tie dyed
Curly, long, straight, short
These kinds of fur are all really great
No matter the size Teddy Bears are cute
Just give me one to call all mine!

# Money
## by Nicholas Kane Griffin

Money, mone, I love money
Money makes me think of honey
It makes me funny
When I think of money, I think of my bunny
I always will dream of money
Money is green
The end of money

# Christmas
## by Taylor Mason

Happy holiday
Christmas is the best time
Christmas trees

# Video Games
## by Enrique Ochoa

Video games are cool
They can have action in them
You have to play on the TV
You can play more than one player

# Moon
## by Diana E. O'Toole

When the day is done
I take the place of the sun
I shine brightly high above
I'm as white as a dove
All my friends including Mars
Have their places with stars
I am the moon and soon I'll be
Floating high for the world to see

# Water
## by Matthew Medrano

Water
So crystal yet so clear
Polluted by people
Filtered by the gills of the fish
How I wish

# Chinese Food
## by Nicholas Rhodes

Yum, yum!
You can eat a buffet
Shrimp, chicken, rice, crab
Pile it up, eat it down
Pile it up, eat it down
Then, get a fortune in a cookie
Then, pay and leave

# Life
## by Bethany Belanger

Life is like
Sitting on a log
Waiting
For someone
To go by

# Dreams
## by Tulsi Mali

Dreams float in the air
There are millions and millions everywhere
Everyone thinks there is no such thing
But way up there in the sky
Little dreams keep on growing
Wherever you look, whatever you see
Dreams float in front of you
Which you cannot see

## A Dangerous Quest
### by Scott Becker

I am a chipmunk, very cute and small
Humans are cutting down my tree which is oh, so tall
My tree is big and brown, one of many in my town
Harm will surely come to my friends and I
If we don't get the humans to stop; but why not try?
So reader, please help me on my dangerous quest
Give it a go and hope for the best
Humans, I think, are very, very mean
Killing fish and mammals and eating them with beans
I am a chipmunk; help me to save my friends
And I can assure you, our friendship will never end
Help me on my dangerous quest, please!


## Penguins In New Zealand
### by Emily van Mulbregt

Penguins in New Zealand are yellow-eyed and blue
They come in from the sea at night but they do not look at you
They waddle, waddle, waddle; up and across the beach
To their sanctuary and nest boxes where there is one for each
They need a sanctuary because they are endangered
I think they are very beautiful so we should protect these birds
(And all the birds of New Zealand)


## Grampy
### by Suzanne Sanford

I was young when he passed away
Sweet little memories and some pictures of him and me
We were always together, side-by-side
He was my best friend
Gray hair, little mustache, plump and round belly
With a comfortable lap to sit on
We had loving memories, burping Fresca
The day he went into the hospital, was the day I'll never forget
He had heart problems
When we got the call saying the he was gone it struck me
I'll never see him again

# Plains
### by Michael Giakoumis

Plains empty like a desert
Not many bison roam the land
Through the dusty trail to California
Bison disappear from most of the land
Plains empty of most living things
Plains empty like a desert

# Colors
### by Tonnie Heggen

I love yellow
Like daisies in a meadow
Deer in the sun
Tiger's eyes of fear
A shell waiting to be washed away
Yellow ~ happiness

# Toothbrush
### by Katelynn Gebo

I think everyone should have a toothbrush, to keep their teeth really white
It's easy to brush up and down to make a smile out of sight!
I really think everyone should have a toothbrush
Any color that you pick
Your teeth will change from dull to bright
It's like a magic trick

# Lunch
### by Alex Gerard

Lunch is fun
That's why I weigh a ton
You can eat whatever you want
That's what I thought
So I brought a Tater Tot
I ran to buy more
But I tripped on a pot
So fiery and hot
Now I have a bad burn
That's why I can't learn!

## Fuzzy Flowers
### by Kaylie Curtis

Fuzzy flowers in the air
Fuzzy flowers in my hair
Fuzzy flowers flying by
Fuzzy flowers say goodbye
In the air, the flowers soar
Purple and fluffy, soft and light
Fuzzy flowers in the air
Oh, I wish that I could be
A fuzzy flower flying free

## My Dreams of the Beach
### by Alyssa Wortz

When I go to sleep, I dream of the beach
That's where I will go when I get old
When I go to sleep, I dream of the beach
I feel the warm breeze blow through the palm trees
Sleep in a hut of bamboo and my heart comes, too
Together we dream, my heart and me, then go to sleep
In the morning I wake to find ice cream and cake
Everything that I want when I dream of the beach
When I go to sleep

## Shopping At the Mall
### by Ashlee Oswald

My friends and I like to go to the mall
Every time we go we have a ball
We shop for clothes and shop for shoes
There is so much it's hard to choose
We go to Icing, we go to Claire's
They sell earrings, all in pairs
They have jewelry, they have rings
They sell all sorts of girly things
When our shopping day is through
We always shout and scream, "Boo-boo"
At home it is not as much fun
Back to the mall we want to run

# Falcons
### by Darrien Williams

Falcons
Are very fast
They are red, white, and black
They are like my favorite team, too
They're good

# You Left Me Here
### by Julie Cokotis

You left me here
You left me with tears and unaccomplished dreams
You left me here
You left me with anger and uninvited sorrow
You left me here
You left me without saying goodbye and no hugs or kisses
You left me here
You left me with questions and they were never answered
You left me here
You left me with pain and confusion
You left me here
Though I do not know why
You left me here

# Knowing When
### by Patricia Breen

I can feel summer's here
When a warm breeze casts around my body
I can taste that summer's here
As a fat, juicy corn on the cob collapses into my mouth
I can hear that summer's here
As tiny peepers outside my window cry in tunes to lullaby me to sleep
I can see that summer's here
When the powerful surge of my campfire is well beyond my head
I can smell that summer's here
As the lively fresh odor, sweet but loving of the blooming tulips
Well resting on the front lawn
But ... I only know it's truly summer when my heart feels that summer's come

# Summary
## by Whitney Albers

Summer is a breeze blowing the worries from you
Summer is a stray sunray tingling your warm skin
Summer is a refreshing glass of lemonade after hard work
Summer is nature singing its song of love, hope and peace
Summer is a swim through life

# Soccer
## by Carly Grit

Is my life
If you get hurt it's life
I love it when I score
It's so fun
I feel happy for
Me and my team for I just
Won the championships
Oh what fun

# The Taste of Nature
## by Jolene Svedin

The water gurgles, trees dance
Sleep comes to deer, moose, and the annoying ants
Wolves howl to announce the rising moon
Before the cold wrath comes, here comes noon
Spring has passed, with its flowers and naps
Perhaps summer tapped
They did not peer
Summer is now here
Grass sway, while deer graze
Forest of mystery and amaze
Leaves turn brown, yellows, and golden too
Summer fun
Has now none
Autumn is new
When summer is so true
When winter the icy tides
The running cold, that hits like knives
Life goes on, while down lives lie

# Soccer Ball
## by Brandon Audet

I am a soccer ball
I am a big, strong ball who looks like a circle with lots of energy
When I feel angry, I can zoom down the field
I am happiest when I am in the middle of the field and no one is kicking me
I say, "Watch out, here I come!" I also tell the players to come and get me
I roll down the field yelling and dodging
People like to kick me or bounce me off their heads
That is a description of me

# Falcons
## by Nicholas Hartle

Flying quickly
Soaring above houses
Sharp eyes
Flying, soaring, seeing
Diving at prey

# Soldiers
## by Damon Zele

Soldiers
Out in the war
Risking their lives in war
Fighting for our country today
Hero

# Forest
## by John Balasco

A forest is a place for nature
Maybe all in one acre
A forest is a place for plants to grow
Without being stepped on by a human toe
A forest may be pretty
But it is no place for a kitty
A forest has trees that are tall
It's hard to find one that's small
A forest is a place we need
It helps animals to find their feed

## Reaching For the Stars
### by Katherine P. Kester

My little brother's peeling laughter blends with the cool air
As I push him on the swing, he seems so happy and free, without a care
"Higher, higher," he shouts, "I want to touch the stars"
His little hand points to the flag waving afar
Then I realize, that if the men had not fought for my country
I would not be having as much fun as this
My little brother would have no stars to reach for
No flag to touch to make his expression bliss
My worries and fears I would wear like a sack
They would stay with me tugging at my back
This is why I salute proudly to the flag on the mast
And thank the brave men of the past


## I Used To Be But Now I Am
### by Kevin Tang

I used to be named for what I do or like
But now people just pick a name, any name for me
I used to be among Taino boys and girls
But now I am among different people from different countries, but no pure Taino
I used to be very trusting and welcomed strangers kindly
But now I am careful and cautious of strangers
I used to be able to paint my body with bold colors
But now I wear only clothes; pants, shirts, and socks
I used to be able to play whenever I wanted
But now I have schoolwork and projects to do
I used to live with people who are gentle and nice
But now I live with some people that are violent and mean
I used to be able to play in the forest all day and night
But now there are not many forests left in the world
I used to be able to walk the Earth barefoot
But now I can't, for people built roads that hurt my feet
I used to hunt animals for food with spears and arrows
But now I just go to the store to buy food that the white man got
I used to be a Taino boy, but now I am not sure who I am

## The Boy's Toy
### by Ryan Delaney

There once lived a boy
Who bought a huge toy
He found he was blind
Suspense blew his mind
He found that it was a huge Coy

## Miracle
### by Nadia East

I hope you know the first time I held you I loved you
I hope you know the first time you smiled I laughed
I hope you know the first time you sat up on your own I told all my friends
I hope you know I love your tiny hands, rosy cheeks, and joyful giggle
I hope you know you're a miracle

## The River
### by Casey Steward

Through the meadow, and past the trees
There is a river better than these
Its water sparkles; it's never hot
Its water is good and there's a lot!
If you drink its water, you'll never thirst
Though next to it is the very worst
Which we are taught not to drink
For it will make us forget to think
The bad water is temptation
Though, the good river is no good here, salvation

## Until I Saw the Mountains
### by Louis B. Shaevel

Until I saw mountains I did not know
That mountains could fall asleep on the clouds
That keep it company every day
I never knew that winter's flakes could kiss the top of mountain caps
Nor did I know before that the sun's blazing embers
Say, "Hello" to it every morning

# Death
## by K. Matthew Brown

Blood like ice; bones like twigs
Skin like paper and hair like ash
Features like the devil
But as calm as a lake in a windless night
Brutal and vile and as bitter as orange rinds
As sudden as a tornado, but as expected as a rainstorm
Always happening, but never wanted

# My Dog Jessie
## by Kasey Tenggren

She is funny, she is cute
She can play the flute
She can sing, she can dance
Kind of like my ants
She likes rubber, she likes plastic
She likes hip-hop, she likes classics
She hates the rain but likes the snow
She runs so fast, don't you know?

# Above and Under
## by Heather Duda

In the sky, there are clouds all around
All shapes and sizes that you can see from the ground
Under the clouds is the land
That has grass, dirt, and even some sand
Under the land is the dirt
With paper and coins and glass that hurts
There are also rocks, sticks, and stones
And pencils and maybe some bones
These are things under and above
Under there are rocks and above there are doves
Also there are flowers and trees
Under and above there is a ton of these living things
There are a lot of creatures all around
Some are noisy and some do not make a sound

# Spring
## by Madelon Roser

By and by the winter's days
The white snow is melting away
So away with the cold numb air
And here comes the hot blast of air
It makes you want to stay in bed all the spring's morn
Then with a pat on your back you finally say no more, I'll get up
When you realize what day it is you will be sad no more
But get up with a smile of course because it's Easter morn


# Blue
## by Jessica Pelletier

Blue is the color of a newborn's eyes
The way they sparkle in the morning skies
The color of a blustery day
Very cold and some things blow away
The color of the morning skies
The time when the bluebirds fly
The color of a happy person
Very happy on a nice blue day


# Winter Nights Performance
## by Megan McHaney

The chilly wind blows as if dismissing the golden sunset
As the cozy sunset disappears, the wind blows again
As if welcoming the snappy cold night
Then the black curtain drops onto the icy milk white snow
Turning it into the huge audience
Then stars begin to sing like a lark and dance as if they were ice-skating
Whenever they stop, the icy wind blows and rattles the trees
As if applauding to the dark night, full of stars dancing and singing
The snow moves as if getting cozy in its icy depth
But when they do, the icy wind blows as if hushing them
There is not a sound as the stars end their singing and dancing
After the performance, the wind blows with its chilly breath
And the trees crackle as if they were applauding with their icy arms
To the wonderful stars and their momentarily freezing and touching performance
But then, the light came as if they were turning on the lights with a switch
And the guests leave, as the sound is cut off
Like a conductor cutting off the music of the beautiful nighttime performance

# Masks
## by Cally Anne LaJeunesse

Acting to a different complexion
Stealing humanity
Cleansing the soul
Hidden beneath the shadows
Stepping into the sun
Blinding the heart
Easing the mind
But inside the illusion
Past the glamour and glitz
Still holds the same heartbeat
The heartbeat of life

# Flag
## by Matt Dellisola

13 stripes
7 red
6 white
50 stars
And some blue
Together we have Red, White, and Blue
Our colors are great for the state
I love Red, White, and Blue

# At Hampton Beach
## by Sarah Roberts

People in the warm, salty water
Splishing, splashing, swish
Rumbling in your stomach, tumbling white waves
Clash, bash, people sprinting into the clear-blue ocean
Swish, swish, people making tall sandcastles
Ding, dong, wake up and feel the red, stinging sunburn
Boing, doing, people passing a bouncy, colorful beach ball
Bang, clang, getting your food at the busy ice cream stand
Snap, snap, "Watch out, a pinching, strong crab is close!"
Caw, caw, white seagulls are flying up above
Pop, pop, the fish's small bubbles have reached the top
Whoosh, whoosh, sea creatures cutting through the water like a knife through butter

# Forgotten
### by Kara Joyce

Hey, where's everyone gone?
I'm all alone on the lawn
Hey, where'd everyone go?
Wait, oh no!
It's Monday!
I'm late


# Spring
### by Theresa Megan Corcoran

The wind is calling; leaves stop falling
Spring is here for part of this year
Gone is the winter gloom; see all flowers bloom
No more need for midnight fire; the pool is our only desire
Kids play outside; grass is so wide
Separated from the cold storms; no more wet snow forms
Skirts and shorts, tents and forts
Roller blading when the sun is fading
Can't resist that sprinkling mist
Rain shower's warmness devourers
Climbing trees, dogs get fleas
Jump roping, no more moping
When the sun goes down, not many frowns
Summer is near, but for now, spring is here!


# Night Sky
### by Tia Kamil Johnson

Sitting on my window sill
The world outside seems very still
The stars outside look so bright
They calm me with their soothing light
Although I had a busy day
I take the time to kneel and pray
To thank the Lord and ask Him why
He loved me so much to give me the night sky

# Moon
## by Paxton McCammon

I went to the moon
On the second of June
I brought a lunch to eat at noon
I saw a crater, big and deep
It would fill a mountain steep
Or ten thousand sheep
I saw some aliens big and wide
Sleeping with some buffalo hide
I couldn't help but laugh inside
When I went up to the moon

# Summer
## by Leslie Barden

A warm gentle breeze begins the day
Summer is beckoning me to come and play
I gaze at the trees, lush and green
The beautiful leaves, smooth and clean
Butterflies gliding by
Gracefully soaring across the sky
Pansies, colorful and bright
Truly summer's a glorious delight

# The Monthly Animals
## by Eliana Agudelo

January is the polar bear, his little ears and his snowy hair
February is the lion cub, for his first love is his first grub
March is the Siamese fighting fish, with his little fins going swish, swish, swish
April is the baby pig; why all he does is lie in a haystack when he isn't that big
May is the beautiful gazelle; she's as great a friend like my buddy, Grisel
June is a leaping lemur; in Madagascar you won't need a heater
July is the toy shih tzu; when it comes to partyin' he knows what to do
August is the little lizard; he's a spitting image of a greenish wizard
September is the kitty cat, while wearing a little black witch hat
October is the hamster, don't ya know? For the little creature knows where to go
November is the cardinal; he has no pain in the abdominal
December is the snow owl, cause he doesn't even like to howl
Back to the polar bear who comes again; each month has its animal friend

## Teddy Bear
### by Nathalie Lavoie

A teddy bear is a cuddly soul
Who listens to every secret murmured in his perky ears
Unless his tot just grew up, and he is lonely and sad
With red eyes, still wet from crying, for he will blabber and bawl
Remembering his grown up tot will make him hum his grown tot's lullaby
So when this teddy strolls
All wet from streams of tears and empty with a lonely heart
Hug him and carry him home to your own tot


## Rock
### by Daniel Wells

Tough like an ox
Smooth like a bowling ball
Thick like an ignorant person's head


## A Long Sea Voyage
### by Justin Ayala

The moon lights the night
The sun lights the day
The food is getting spoiled
The drinks are getting warm
The waves keep on swaying
The ship keeps on rocking
I'm beginning to feel a little sick
The captain is well and determined
I hear the crew shouting
And I am very shy
I smell the salty sea air
And not the clean air, as I'm used to
All I see is water
Not any land to sight
I don't think I will make it
For the voyage is not stopping
I would like to be with my mother
But I think we're lost at sea
I still keep hoping that our voyage will stop at land
And then I hear, "Land Ho!" and our journey comes to an end

## Indians
### by Ariana Fiorello

Where are they now?
The caring
The hunters
The colorful
The brave
The reddish-brown skin
The cherishing and treasuring
The peaceful
The ones who lived on the prairie
The ones who lived in teepees, adobes, and soddies
Heaven


## F-22 Raptor
### by Cody Pitchios

Jet screeching
Flying by clouds
Missiles soaring
Making massive destruction
Flying into war


## Poetry
### by Tadela Tedemet

Poetry to me is a voice that sings with ability
Shows when you need sensitivity
And tells your thoughts gracefully
As birds chirp, and babies cry
Poetry can lift you high
Makes you laugh and makes you sing
For me, poetry can do anything
When you need a calming voice
Poetry should be your choice
When the sun sets in the evening sky
Poetry will get you through the night
When the sun comes up, but doesn't shine very bright
Poetry will show you the light
So what is poetry to me?
Poetry is everything

## She Loves Me Lots
### by Jade St. Paul

I had a teacher who loved me lots
She told me to draw a picture of flowerpots
I took a flight in an airplane
I came back to school again
What a blast; no school today
I forget, it's my birthday!
I go back home, my teacher is there
What a surprise, it's my mother!


## The Cat
### by Ashley Beville

One afternoon I thought I saw a cat
I thought it looked like it was fat
Maybe it's a baseball player
Then it got grayer
Then it hit a ball with a big bat


## Laughter
### by Samantha Owens

Laughter of children
Within the blooming meadow
Laughing, just laughing


## Beaches
### by Jacqueline Abdallah

Swimming in the beautiful ocean
Walking in the soft sand
Surfing waves twelve feet high
Making exquisite sandcastles
Fishing for enormous stripers
Searching tide pools for orange crabs
Playing pickle on a cloudy morning
Missing the fun when I go home!

# Things That Inspire Creativity
## by Alexis Rodriguez

Things that inspire creativity
Are projects that are competitive, even for me
What I mean is that I need more beans
To beat the person in front of me

# Ladybug
## by Sarah Beatty

Ladybug
I'm caught
Let me go
Please now
Your hands open
I am free

# The Clown
## by Kapua Sportsman

There once was a very sad clown
He wanted to turn upside down
But nobody let him
So he changed his name to Tim
And now he wears a big fat frown

# School
## by Chanta Payne

I think school is fun
It is a really fun place to learn things, new things
My favorite subject is Science
I just like it; it is really fun
I have a lot of friends at school
I had a good teacher
Right now, I have an awesome teacher
Her name is Ms. Wang
I love my principal; I love my teacher
I love my friends; I love everything about my school

# Clock
### by Kasie Tucker

I have a face and two hands
I can be old or young
I cry when you are pulling my hands
I feel sad when people switch my time
When you change my time, I ask you, "What time is it?"
All I do is hang on the wall and spin my wheels all day long
Sometimes I feel like I am going too fast
Sometimes I feel like I am going too slow
When it's 12:00 I shout
"Hooray it's time to eat!" Or "It's time to sleep!"


# The Night Before Hanukkah
### by Ryan Fink

'Twas the night before Hanukkah, when all through the camp
All the new fallen snow made the city quite damp
The wrapped presents were put in the mail
In hope that Ryan, would get a big blue whale
The children were lighting the candles with care
While saying the prayer they covered their hair
And mama wanted us to join the song
So we all started to sing along
The candles burned the whole night long
The next day more children joined the song
So they lit the candles once again
Now the children were as many as ten
It was the third day of Hanukkah we celebrate
And December first was the date
Yet when more and more presents finally came
Four of my friends got video games
Five of my friends got fifty dollars
And some got shirts without collars
The people told the story with knights
When the war was over, there was oil for one night
Days passed, the eighth day the candles were still lit
Till the menorah was ruined and all was quiet
And that is why we celebrate this holiday
So dreidel we shall play, hey!

# Tornadoes
## by Austin Hillyard

Tornadoes can be scary
They can be rough
Anything in its path it will bury
Tornadoes are usually very tough
In addition, very difficult to describe
F-scales, there are five
Each can make many trails
Each tornado will most likely thrive
Each fits in one of the F-scales
An F-5 can tear a house to shreds
A tornado may occur at any degree
Tornadoes, there are many kinds
The kinds that throw debris
The kinds with many winds
Some kinds can even throw a house
Some only a mouse!

# Architecture
## by Dana Mazurowski

Buildings big and buildings small
Architects designed them all
Whether fancy or plain
Old or new, they remain
Architecture is an art
Use your brain; use your heart
To design
Be creative in your mind
To build
Make sure you're skilled
To plan
Believe you can
Do not wait to create!
Create a structure that's unique
Colorful and sleek
Beautiful buildings, big or small
Architects designed them all!

# The Picture
## by Maria Maier

The picture in the gallery of my shady, sands-of-time heart
Ink blotted with red-life-burn looked harmonious in my point of dream tune
It's prettier-than-my-eyes deep blue shade of sky
Froze me in ice crystallism for a period of time that seemed like eternal darkness
For us – my heart and I
But the prettiest part of young painted "Charming"
Is his radiant moon scar on the eye of all ideas
The protector of the keeping brain – the forehead of life
Probably his serious face held his body steady, before toppling over
Like a blast of sonic fire from changeling side of airy "colora"
I see in him from the outside of his mellow suit, no – the opposite of mellow
Strong and hearty, the likes of which I have never seen
And usually he makes me feel like the eerie, but safe sound of a cold night
In my cozy Tundra, hidden deep in my mind of courageous emotionism
For me, myself and I, most of all heavenism, to say, heavenism
Faster, faster the clock ticks, night is over and day in my mind has come
To a swell start of a brand-new imaginative thought
I wish to share with erosions and tough emotion to "painting"
The fastest race of blood zips through me when I look at the painting
Him – and I feel a piercing pain-ache through my body, that asks me a question
To which I always mercilessly reply to stop the pain - "Elohim, Elohim"
Is what I reply to the spear of pain
Quieter I think at night - I walk to painting in my thoughts
And plop into a puddly mess of his world – I am on a canvas
Painted by my "Charming", my creator, but my decider chose me as his dream
And I chose him as opposite-same his thoughts
My, my quietest heavenly man as quoting Socrates and all
The others of my take-off flight to his art world, of my painting
I cannot take my eyes off, his picture floating
In two pools of liquid tilled "my eyes" by creator
Thicker than all my imaginative Heroism, a picture of my savior, my Hercules
In disguise as a simple country life general, but oh-so-much more than that
Try to truly understand my emotion that no one can relate to me
Through poetical painting man, I do not truly know him
As either a dynamical human or a painting, nevertheless a shot of dear
Thickest man I see, my "Charming," I live my word for you as lies and truths
I turn away from endless creator - he, my painting is of my loving dear father
And I, young Eva, I am speaking of God

## Untitled
### by Faisal Rashid Wasti

There was a lady who had a baby
The baby was so funny
The baby was so crazy
The baby was trying to get honey
So the baby could get bunny


## What a Tree Knows
### by Andrew Hebert

The old tree in the backyard, it's been standing there forever
Never moving and can't fight back
Some of its bark has been torn off
Rain makes the tree feel sad and so does the wind
I visit this tree when it needs help
It sits there like a wounded knight who can't sit up
This tree is elderly and knows all the birds around and all the sounds
If he could talk, he could answer every question
He knows the sky and the ground
He is lonely, but one day he fell over like a bowling pin
All of his feelings and thoughts would be lost forever


## When I Got Dotty
### by Kortney Lovett

When I got Dotty she was in a towel
I was so happy she was so cute
I picked her up and let Bear sniff her
She was so skinny and we fed her eight bowls of milk and five bowls of dog food
And would growl at Bear when he was near it
That night I slept with her; I kept her warm and she kept me warm
We played all day and night and I slept outside in the garage with Bear and Dotty
We taught them to shake, roll over, sit, dance and jump
I loved Dotty
When she got ran over I was so sad
I screamed and cried and I couldn't sleep, eat, or drink
I was so sad, I stayed home that day; I stayed home and cried
Dotty

# Untitled
### by Christopher Lee Bishop

There once was a man from Sheer
He could smell the scent of a man's fear
He played a perfect game of poker
He had a reputation for being a joker
He has even been known to make grown men shed a tear


# School
### by Logan Remling

"No," is all they ever say!
They never say, "Oh, yes!"
They always say, "No, you can't
Doodle
Sleep in class
Listen to music
Run in the hall
No food
No dogs or cats
Only obedience"
And this boring old thing called ... "Work!"


# Thankful
### by Samantha Quinn

I am a Queen
Rich with happiness, not with money, but with feelings and my family
I am a rabbit
With a burrow to come home to when I don't know what to do
There is still one thing I know, I can always come home
I am a seed
Being fed by my gardener, growing to be healthy
Knowing that when I am hungry, my gardener will feed me
I am a wolf with a pack
We care for and help each other; I know my pack will always be there for me
I am a thank you card
Thanking God for life

## The Bee
### by Mahlik Brown

Going up a tree
Getting nectar from plants
Flying all over the place, gingerly about their work
And being exceedingly, being chivalry

## Untitled
### by Elena C. Hellums

Finely stitched and white
Head when out of sight
My proud delight

## Coco
### by Dustin C. Mathews

Coco will bark at you; she will bark at your friend too
She won't bark at me because I don't make her pay a fee
Coco is jumpy, way more than me
She is happy with my other dog; she likes to take a jog
Coco is protective; she is a detective
Coco is a dog; she likes to play in the bog
Coco was bought, at least we thought
She thought so also because we told her so
Coco likes to play; she would like to play in the hay
If we had any; maybe we should call Benny

## Best Friends
### by Autumn Berryman

Best friends are always right beside you
And you know you'd be there for them, even if it takes forever
You know you're able to fit your best friends in
Even if you don't realize that you help each other every day
You're always gonna be the same in every way

## Books, Books, Books
### by Jada Petersen

There are so many books around
I can't even find the one I want
The one I want, but the one I want is nowhere to be found
The reason I want my book is because I write in that my very big dark secrets
That no one knows about

## Glider Plane
### by Alexis Ortega

Flying high
Looking through clouds
No sound
Wing over wing
Whispers of life

## The Dictionary
### by Emma Clarkson

C ... G ... M ... R ...
Resemble, resent, reserve
Response, rest, result
Retrieve, reveal, review
When will I find what I want?

## Untitled
### by Audrey Svedin

I may have a short life
You may have a long life
But if we work together
We may have a lot of fun
You may live in a castle
Or you may live on the streets
I'll always lend you a helping hand
Even though you're different from me
So if we stand together
We may just make it through the battles of life
Having a joyous time as we go
We all are going to the same place when we die
So why don't we just respect our differences and say, "You're doing just fine"

# Untitled
## by Dustin Winters

In January, my brother says the snow must go
But he actually says it in woe
In March it turns into summer
Maybe I'll plant a cucumber
In April there are many showers
That last for hours
In May the weather is warm and sunny
Maybe you could find some honey
In June it's so hot
It feels like 1000 watts
In July it will be steaming
And you'll be dreaming of cold
In August it will be sizzling
And you'll wish it was drizzling
In September it's cool
And you're going to school
And all the rest
Are all the best

# I Love Nature
## by Kristopher Leblanc

Nature makes me relax
And nature sounds beautiful
Take time to listen to nature
Use your time to watch nature
Read about nature
End hurting nature

# Baseball
## by Amanda Judd

Balls get hit hard
A lot of times I pitch
Some people throw hard
Everyone gets nervous when they pitch
Big hits in the air
A lot of people get out
Lots of different people play first base
Lots of people cheer

# Peace
### by Meghan Smith

rePose
frEedom
Amity
reConciliation
amnEsty

# Friendship
### by Kelsea Millie Bowers

Fun
Remember
Irresistible
Easy
Nice
Deep
Sharing
Happy
Immense
Polite

Friendship is better than anything else
But you can't just think of yourself

# The Water
### by Jessica Stratton

Windy
A flower
Temperature
Evaporation
Rainy

In the daylight
Sunny

Cloudy
One snowflake
On the grass
Life

## Snowy Midnight
### by Arica Holloway

Something floats to the ground
Nobody heard it
Only the squirrel
What a night this was! The squirrel wished
You could see it too

Moon showed her face
In the snowy midnight
Deep in the trees owls will spy
Nesting
In the ground
Gophers protect their babies
Hopping rabbits hide in
Their holes in the dirt

## My Friend
### by Taylor Rhodes

Likeable
Attitude
Unique
Righteous
Entelligent
Nice

Super
Excellence
Awesome
Loving
Yes, it is true!

# The Things That I'm Thankful For
## by Omar A. Alvarez, Jr.

A for another day God has given me to live
B for the beginning of a new quarter at school
C for the huge Caribbean Sea that I have been in
D for the delicious food I eat everyday
E for the great entertainer I am
F for the fresh water I drink
G for the Great Wall of China
H for how many days to Thanksgiving
I for how independent I am
J for my friend Jonathan
K is for the kitchen my family cooks in
L is for the leader, Martin Luther King
M is for my favorite planet, Mars
N for the national anthem of America
O for the best Olympic games
P for the Pledge of Allegiance at school
Q for Tom Brady, the best quarterback
R for the American patriot, Paul Revere
S for the sweet sound of the saxophone
T for the Spanish American dance, the tango
U for the unusual things I do
V for the vets that help the animals
W for where I live
X for Malcolm X
Y for the Yankees losing the playoffs
Z for the zipper in my jacket

# A Lincoln-Eliot Poem
### by Tyler Connell

Lovely spring flowers in the springtime
Indigo skies in spring and summer
Nice teachers to learn from
Cool friends to hang out with
Outside for recess after lunch
Lunch in a lively cafeteria
Nice playground equipment to play with

Elegant principal to lead the school
Lovely lunch ladies
Into computer work projects
Out of sight P.E. classes
Time to learn

# My Magical Letters
### by Anaissa Nunez

Amazing
Nuts
Adorable
Idiot
Sassy
Sugar
Annoying

New
Unbelievable
Noun
Easy
Zebra

Chené Benoit

*A multi-talented honor student
who now calls sixth grade home,
Chené has won awards for
Reading, Computer Skills, Math,
Social Studies, and now, Poetry.
Even with all the accolades,
she still lists her family
as the most important thing in her life.*

# Mommy
## by Chené Benoit

I am blessed with an angel
Who knows how I like my tea
My guardian angel and special friend
Who watches over me
She hugs me when I'm sad
Even when I make her mad
She calls me her miracle
But I'm the one who feels lucky
God sent me a guardian angel
That I can call Mommy

Brittany Cormier

Brittany is currently a sixth grade student,
and when she isn't writing award winning poetry,
she can be found in dance class
where she studies both ballet and tap.
She also enjoys arts and crafts,
and playing with her two dogs,
Chelsea and Foster.

Daddy's Heart
by Brittany Cormier


When I slide my little palm into his
I feel the whole world stop
A shield of protection glides around me
I cradle my head into his chest
The constancy of his heart beats with my own
Even as I grow
I will be his baby
In my daddy's heart
I know he loves me!

# Division II
# Grades 6-7

## Black and White
### by Loan Pham

When I look out the window, all I see is black and white
There is so much hatred that needs to be wiped
Every person can be different
From people who are happy, to ones who are homeless
But in everyone's soul, there is always selfishness
We should be having peace, not thinking of only ourselves
We should be thankful for everyone else
Soldiers throughout the nation are trying to fight
So there's no more hatred that needs to be wiped


## Rare
### by Emily Russo

Someone very special
Someone very rare
Someone you can't find
On the ground or in the air
A gem, your good friend
Always having time to spare
Only one place to be found
In your heart and in your care


## Who You Are
### by Erin Benotti

Your strong arms catch me when I fall
Your sense of humor brightens up my day
Your smile tells me everything is going to be okay
The actions from your heart let me know you care
Your sharp eye picks out details that make the world more beautiful
Your ever-lasting endurance of love follows you and those who you share it with
The days I don't spend with you, I carry a hole in my heart
I feel complete when you're around; your guidance is always cherished
Thank you for being who you are
For this, Dad, I am ever grateful

# Friends
## by Althea Sylvia

Friends are always there when you're down
That's why you need them all around
Having friends of different backgrounds is wonderful
That's what makes friendships so colorful
I have one friend that loves to dance
At the end of every song she does her stance
Another friend is a horse lover
She loves them as if they were her own brother
My other friend is funny and smart
She's also great at art
Another friend loves sports
She loves them so much that her room should be a basketball court
But there's a lot of friends I know
And yet there's not enough room to show
But they all know I care
And that's the reason why I'm there


# The Life
## by Samantha Russell

Because of you, I no longer
Can create the view I've seen before
Down my body and my mind
Eerie sounds come alive
Living life becomes a chore
In this world of food and bore
And when there comes a day
It might all fade away
Losing faith day by day
Most times in a way
No one knows
But it's here to stay
Quiet now, the sound no more
Rest now, before the day
When it might all fade away
Tough out, hurt inside
Upside down my life has turned
Very soft you whisper now
It'll be alright ... for now

## Animals, Animals
### by Blair Hennington

How I love animals
Short, tall, big, fat
Animals are the sweetest
Cats, dogs, pigs, and horses, too
All kinds of animals are waiting for you
Baths and brushing might be work
But it all pays off with love
Oh, oh how I love animals! Yea!


## The Assassin
### by Josh Martin

The Cat
Ferocious and stealthy
Pounces and devours
Remorselessly
A Tiger


## Greece
### by Connor H. Gallagher

There is a mountain Olympus
Its peeks were very high
There are houses every where
Their names are Greeks
It was very high
The mountains are steep
It hurts to climb
The mountains hurt your feet
They own old farms
They grow grapes
They grow olives
They don't come in shapes
They were surrounded by water
The people don't have great land
The Pindus Mountains cover the land
The kids play in the sand
They grow crops
They grow flowers
The crops grow fast
The people take showers

# Happiness
### by Victoria Ruth Bean

Happiness
On a sunny day the trees are still until the wind blows
And the shadows of the branches sway in the wind
Like a child in their bed tossing and turning, experiencing a nightmare
Then all is still, as they sit bolt up right in their bed, sweating with fear
As if it has just poured and washed all the happiness out of them
But then the clouds roll away and sunlight appears
Drying your face of all sweat and tears
Happiness


# Tid Bit Tank
### by Stephen Long

The pink fairy armadillo
Plated and miniscule
Burrows and blemishes
Slightly
The Earth


# Perpetual Winter
### by Katie Bousquet

The shimmery gold haze of fall time makes way
To the glimmering silvery daze of winter time once again
No more crimson colors lining the harvest basket
Now it is covered in the angel white snow, so pure and untouched
Sparkling enticingly at all who see it
Countless days under these dull colored, clouded skies – vanilla skies
No more gold snuggled autumnal dreams for me
But now that winter has come, I must say
That now my dreams are distant and cold, dull colored like a silvery crescent moon
Such moon on wintry day, lost in perpetual winter land bliss
But all the same lost, lost like a November rain
I miss the rippled jades and chocolate browns of autumn
All colors unite in the trees at this time of year
Now only winter snow is here
Giving antique whites and luscious colors of the natural palette a new name
Lost in this mystical land of icicles and snow
Perpetual winter land bliss for months on end
Until spring's song returns for me in warmer times ahead

# Papa
## by David Nassoura

I see a peaceful person going to a better place
I smell all the flowers that have been left for him
I touch his cold hand; his fingers are white like snow
It tastes sad, but good, to know he is in a happy place
I hear his voice in the distance telling me words of wisdom
He is still with us in our hearts and in Heaven


# Ode To a Pencil
## by Stasha O'Callaghan

You use it to get your ideas onto paper
Its golden-rod color and small pink eraser
The mundane gray tint of the words that are written
Can be brought to life if the word choice is fittin'
Pencils have many uses like drawin' and sketchin'
With a number 2 pencil you'd answer a test question
The purpose of pencils may seem quite clear
But without this contraption writing could disappear
So simple a tool as this you may not seem to miss
But ponder all its uses, see you'd be remiss to dismiss


# Goodbye
## by Victoria M. Pitts

My cheeks burned like fire
The tears I couldn't hold back
The memories of you I hold dearest
The pain I try to push back
The pictures still bring back memories
Sleeping is hard every night
Sometimes I have to remember
It's time for you to take flight
Spread your wings and soar
High up in the sky
Precious little angel
It's time to say goodbye

# Gray Rose
## by Leah Rothchild

Lights went off when my father was born
A faceless, yet beautiful child to hold
Where roses are gray and features flat
A seemingly colorless world
Wrinkled hands, tenuous eyelids
Stumbling feebly into obstacles
Dog whimpers, bitter gasps of horror
Tumbling through the wrong door
Fragile head smacking concrete
Like gunshots in a rhythm gone amiss
Flight of stairs now her rocky cliff
A piercing shelterless silence
Motionless on concrete floor
Rushing to her aid down steep cement steps
Traumatic trembling as she takes a breath
Doesn't slow anyone's rapid heartbeat
She learned way back when that her only survival
Was to just let go and hang loose, when falling into darkness
Yet I know through her detachment her internal rose can beam again
With the magnificent red she has inside


# I Am
## by Ben Campbell

I am as calm and rough at the same time as the ocean
I am like a rabid dog when I get mad
I am like an unstoppable hurricane when I get mad
I am a purring cat when I am happy, easy to please
I am a bulldozer when someone gets in my way, clearing them out of my path
I am like a quiet river at school, staying quiet and out of the way
I am like a bull when I play basketball, becoming intense with every passing second
I am a grain of sand in the world, just living with everyone else
I am a day with rain and dark skies when I get upset
I am like a cloudless day when I am happy
I am like a warm sunny day to those around me

## Forget and Remember
### by Ariana Lynn Payne

Forget his name; forget his face
Forget his kiss and warm embrace
Forget the love you two once knew
Remember now, there's someone new
Forget the time you two once shared
Forget the fact that he once cared
Forget him when he played his song
Forget the time you got along
Forget how close you two once were
Remember now, he's chosen her
Forget the time he called on the phone
Forget the time he left you alone
Forget the time he was your dream come true
Remember now she loves him too
Forget the thrill when he walked by
Forget the time he made you cry
Forget the time he said your name
Remember now, things aren't the same
Forget the time he held your hand
Forget the sweet things if you can
Forget the time he said, "I will leave you never!"
Remember now, he's gone forever


## The Soldier In the Shadow
### by Alexzandra Eve Lizama

In the horizon, I see a silhouette of a person
Their identity hidden by the falling darkness
I duck behind an old willow tree, for fear he will see me
I don't know who he is or what he will do to me
Because in these times of war, you can trust no one
As he gets closer, I see he is holding a bayonet
I stare in disgust
He is a British soldier who thinks we shouldn't be a free country
Go away redcoat, I think hopefully, so I can go home and go to bed
But it's too late, he caught me
He drags me away onto a ship and leaves me there to die

# If I Wasn't Me
## by Christine Grayton

If I wasn't me I would be someone else
With dark brown hair and round green eyes and clothes a different style
I'd be shorter than I am right now and I would be writing this poem
In a different form with different words and it would be a little like this ...
If I wasn't me I'd be someone else
With dirty blonde hair and jolly brown eyes and clothes a different style
I'd be taller than I am right now and that would be me and is


# Life
## by Sean Rush

Life is a beautiful thing
What is a better thing
Is knowing that you brought it to life
And that is the best of them all


# Angel
## by Ty'Ara Davis

Sometimes, I feel like I don't belong anywhere
And it's gonna take so long for me to get somewhere
Sometimes, I feel so heavy-hearted and I can't explain 'cause I'm so guarded
But that's a lonely road to travel and a heavy load to bear
And it's a long, long way to Heaven, but I gotta get there
Can you send me an angel? Please send me an angel to guide me
Sometimes, I feel like a door with no key
And all the answers are locked away in me and they're hard to find
Especially, when I feel lost and so blind
But that's a lonely road to travel and heavy load to bear
And it's a long, long way to Heaven, but I gotta get there
Can you send me an angel? Please send me an angel to guide me
'Cause I don't wanna feel like a dove with no wings
And I don't wanna know what a heart of stone sings
'Cause that's a lonely road to travel and a heavy load to bear
It's a long, long way to Heaven, but I gotta get there
Can you send me an angel? Please send me an angel to guide me ...

# Freedom
## by Amber Bigelow

Has anyone ever asked you what you think freedom means?
Have you ever asked yourself what freedom means?
I ask myself almost everyday
Then, I think about a life of freeness for me
I asked myself what the free in freedom means
Freedom means sitting on top of a mountain in the valley
Lying in the grass with the hot summer breeze on my neck
Freedom means drinking from a crystal blue stream, next to a meadow of flowers
And being on the other side of the world from civilization
Freedom means no drought, no famine
No drugs that can cause bodily harm and a cure for cancer and AIDS
Freedom means not worrying about diseases or viruses
Not needing medication and living out in the open
Freedom means watching a herd of cattle graze in the grass
Or naming a land yours, your own
Freedom means sleeping under the starlit sky gazing at the moon wondering
And thinking about what my purpose is in life and why you were ever created
Until you fall asleep in the heat of the dry, pale sky
Freedom means not having any rules and living with the animals in the wild
Running with the Black Panther till night fall
And resting with the White Tiger till daybreak
Freedom means having more than one favorite thing in life, to try something new
Freedom means to be able to watch the paint dry on a freshly new painted wall
And to not be judged on your first impression, but on your second
Freedom means jumping off a cliff and floating safely and slowly to the bottom
Without any injuries except the windburn formed around your lips
And your watering eyes
Freedom means caring for the environment and banning poachers
From areas where endangered species live
Freedom means, "Not being judged by the color of your skin
But the content of your character"
Freedom means to be treated equally
I am not just talking about humans but other creatures, too
Freedom means living in the mountains and living until you are 70
And being able to support the others that you love in their times of need
Freedom means speaking from your heart
And not thinking about what you are truly saying
Freedom means no time limits in the day or night
And coming and going when I please
Freedom means no ruler and no we, just me, myself, and I
Freedom means being you, not showing off
And feeling whole and pure all at the same time
Freedom has more than one meaning as you can see

# Judgment
## by Alexis Garrett

Kids nowadays
Hardly ever say a word of praise
Kids are afraid
Of what others have to say
Copying others' every move, watching their every step
Even if it means they'll have to do something that they'll soon regret
I chose the road less traveled, the path others are afraid to take
But I know my image isn't fake; I also know my reputation isn't nearly at stake
Don't be afraid of what other kids might say
Stand out! Scream your name! Come on, be brave!
Popularity is just a phase of insecurity
But only your heart is the true fountain of purity
Don't judge and be courageous, and that should be enough!


# Why
## by Margaret Neisess

You sit there and laugh while I stand back
You steal their money and their lunch
Then give them and their friends a hurtful punch
I go to the office after geography
On the way you threaten me
You take their books and rip them up
Because when they see you they just give up
As I hold back and wonder why
You stroll around and make kids cry
I rest in my place and do not chase
As you hit people in the face
At lunch with your friends you laugh at kids while walking by
Then all of a sudden, you are alone and wonder why

# Black History
## by Chelsea Harding

As you have seen me
For now I'm gone
I seek your death
For I've seen you beaten
Sticking up for your freedom, your children, your life
How I can seek you truly?
As you float away
As you cross the river as you forgot day by day
For now you are gone
And memories fade away
Our dear children beat and broke, float away
As I watch them in their death
By a whip of pain
As I've seen you from heaven
As for now we all meet again


# What Could Happen
## by Cassandra Arthur

What could happen...
When the world fell apart, or when everybody died
When families went against each other, when feelings always die
If hearts are always broken and lies are always said
What could happen if we never spoke
If we never fell in love, if we always stayed apart
If we never live to see what has just begun
If we never get married that would be a shame
Or if we never see each other
If we always cry, if we never laugh again
If we always sigh, if we only listen, if we ignore
If we see beyond each other, or if we don't bother
If we hold hands, or if we kiss
If we come back together, maybe the world will come too?

# Red
### by Jenna Hoffman

Red is a rose with dew on its tips
It is the color of a baby girl's lips
Red is the battlefield after the fight
Red are the eyes of a stranger at night
Red can be snarly, scary, and mean
It can be calming, gentle, unseen
Red is the color of courage and might
The anguishing fate of a wound burning bright
Red is the ruby gem, bursting with shine
Red is the soul, cherished, loving, divine

# Blender Meet Heart
### by Felicia Goodwin

I've already told him
I hope he hasn't forgot
Waiting for his response
My heart has stopped
Waiting …waiting
Waiting for him to say
I'm sorry, but I don't like you that way
I'd hate for him to say that
That's how it's gonna be
There isn't gonna be a him and me
I can't get my hopes up
It's way too fast
I know our being friends is past
Now I'm getting a serious doubt
This thought is turning me inside out
I'm biting my lip
It's starting to bleed
I hope he's not trying to tease
I've tried too hard to be patient
It's getting to me
Why can't he just speak?
I hope he's not trying to sneak away
I'll just have to wait another day

# The Golden Mom
## by Meghan Dionne

Whenever I am around my mom it never rains
Because when she steps out the door and smiles
She lights up the world with sunshine
In my mom's eyes, she may just be a mom
But in mine, she is an angel brought from above
My mother always says that being a mom is the best job you can ever have
But being a daughter of hers is the best you can ever get
When you look into her eyes, the goodness from her heart shines right into yours
Spending time with my mom is like a sweet remedy
I cherish every moment of our time together
I look forward to every morning because it is a new memory I can hold
My mother means the world to me and that love will never change
I have learned that it grows deeper every day
As life goes on I will learn every delicate trait
And the love that exists between a mother and a child
Someday I hope to be the one reading this poem about me


# As I Went A-Walking
## by Ellida Cornavaca

Through the woods
As I and man's best friend went a-running
Through the woods we looked so cunning
As I looked over my shoulder and into the brush
My palms were sweating and my mind was pondering
Thoughts bounced in my head; on and on they went a-wondering
The wind whistled on a day so crisp
I said, "Tis the wind, playing games with my head!
As day is bright and autumn's red!"
I longed for it and wanted like a man with his carpentry
I wanted it to be just the woods and me
I love what I have and I've come to appreciate the things that I've lost
One thing I won't lose is the woods sorrel and moss

# At Last
## by Jasmyn Franklin

Note by note the music flows, like a stream upon a hill
Dreams and faith keep me going, the only thing they can't kill
Sweat rolls down my brow, turning into tears
Lurking behind every corner, I start to feel my fears
Running away I can't escape the sorrow or the pain
Holding on to my songs so dear, it's hard to stay sane
This night is very different; I have no master whipping me
Not like the years that have passed, I am finally free!

# Life
## by Christina Mitchell

Life is harsh; life is mean
And so it pays you back for all the stupid things that go on today
Your heart tells you not to, but your so called friends say otherwise
Which is good?  Which is bad?
They don't know about all the harsh times I've had
About the harsh times everyone has had
No matter if it is yesterday, today, or tomorrow
Life is harsh; life is mean
And so it pays you back for all the stupid things that go on everyday

# Destiny
## by Julia Amero

You may think you're a smart spender but that's just what you are told
You walk around with gum on your shoe and wonder when life will unfold
You dream away your free time, you want to live life right now
You refuse to work your life away; so instead you sing, dance and laugh aloud
You spend your summers like in the movies, you don't mind if you're a little late
Until the day you bump into a man that says "No ... it's not luck, it's fate"
Then you start thinking, what will my life be like?
Will you grow to be rich and famous? Or live the simple life instead
You think of what your life was and will be; while sitting in your office all grown up
You remember what that old man said "It's not luck ... it's fate ... it's Destiny"

# Ray Charles
## by Corey Medovich

The music flows beat by beat
I can feel the pedals beneath my feet
The dancing crowd is cheering me on
When I play my famous song
If I take a walk in the park
I open my eyes; the world is dark
They say I'm no good, because I'm blind
But if you hear me, I'm worth your time
Listen with your ears and open your heart
My name is Ray Charles and the party is about to start

# Nothing But Flying
## by Nina Thompson

Nothing in my hands, nothing at my feet, nothing on my face
No one speaks to me
I look lonely at the skies, wishing I was flying!
I wish I had wings, I wish I had brains
Just smart, not stupid, just flying, not walking
Just loving, not hating, just flying
Not coloring, but drawing, not friends, but relationships
Not worshiping, but praising
Flying

# Apple Crisp
## by Kate Margulis

I sniff the air and take in the scent
While I watch my mom as she spoons this delight onto my plate
I smell it, all the spices drifting, floating up into my nose
My mom puts the plate down in front of me
Tempting me to shove it into my mouth like a dog
But instead, I stay human and pick up my fork
Preparing to take a bite of the golden brown, slightly burnt treasure
Finally, the treat is in my mouth; I am overwhelmed with joy
I am amazed by the wonders of this food and my mouth waters
Waiting, waiting for the next spoonful of heaven

# The Pear Tree and Old Man
## by Josh Baker

Old Man once told me stories everyday
Stories that showed bravery and courageousness, I must say
Under the pear tree, memories to my grave
The shade, the fruit of which it gave
Old Man spoke; the breeze stirred lightly as he began
Telling a sad story about a lonely man
The man fought to live, that was his only goal
As everyday for him was gathering coal
The coal dust gathered in his blood-shot eyes
His life was all just depressing lies
Coal scratched into his face, memories that would not be fair
The wind brushed my soft dark skin, as I went for another pear
I went back to the pear tree 60 years later, hoping it would still be
Tense, sadness was building inside me
I heard a sound in the wind as it ran
A sentence pulsing in my heart: "Old Man"


# Candy
## by Filipe Dourado

Sweet candies serve me right
When the craving comes at night
Creeping down my house stairs
I look and seek for Gummy Bears
I grab the bears with both hands
And shove them down my healthy glands
But somehow, I'm still not satisfied
With the growls my tummy makes inside
Snickers, Reese's, and Musketeers
Are always on my mind these years
But apples, bananas, oranges, and pears
Are the reasons for all my fears
My mom tells me to always eat right
But I always eat the sweet stuff that's in my sight
I love Kit Kats, Hershey's and Starburst
Because whichever I see is the one I eat first
Candies are addictive and cause much pain
But you know what they say, "No pain, no gain"
I think I've had enough of this game
Only because my mom is coming up the stairs to take away my candy cane

# Spectacular
## by Mary Lou Martin

The rainbow
Sparkling and elegant
Glows and sways
Calmly
The Neon Tetra

# Carrots
## by Alejandro I. Theodosiou

Carrots are as long as the world
Carrots are as wide as the trunk of a tree
They're as tall as the Eiffel Tower
They're as orange as pumpkins
They're as wrinkled as my grandmother's face
Carrots are as dry as the Sahara Desert
Carrots are as crunchy as bones

# Life Is Like
## by Akiyo Nishimiya

Life is like a stream; you never know what's ahead
Because one day you might fall dead
Like a waterfall does
Your path winds far, through mountains, plains, and maybe one day the drain
Like a river
Many may not like you, yet others like the seal
Like to have the deal of living in both land and ocean
You have feelings, like when you're mad
Then soon you feel like you've done something bad
Lakes and ponds are just the same when storms come by their way

# Untitled
## by Ross Carley

The herbivore
Both pouched and powerful
Grazes and leaps
Gracefully
A kangaroo

# Frustration
### by Nicholas Yordy

Frustration is a huge fire, constantly looking for fuel to grow
Burning through all shreds of peace, until you extinguish it
Frustration is a speeding gazelle, racing through your body
Ignoring all common solutions, only making it worse
Frustration is an eraser, erasing your self-confidence
Wiping away your self-esteem, only pointing out your mistakes


# Broken Friendship
### by Lauren Hamrick

Oh, I can't stand her!
I tingle when she's around
That backstabber got what she deserved
I can't talk to her, but I remember all the good times we had
All the sleepovers, trick-or-treating together
When I think I hate her, I can't stop thinking I've caused this
You see, friendship is forever, so why are we at war?
I want to talk to her; I want to figure out what went wrong
Now that I think about it, I don't think I can go on knowing she's not my best friend
I have to have my broken friendship repaired


# I Am the Child
### by Kourtney Lewis

I am the child
The child who everybody puts last in line, but should be first
I am the child
The child who has been hated because I can do things better than they can
I am the child
The child who has been looked at as conceited
I am the child people say, "You're all that," but I am really not
I am the child
The child who can sing, dance, and step
I am a black, beautiful child
You can tell me I'm not but I don't care what you say
I am the child
Who is always last who should be first

# Untitled
## by Kevin Reed

The storm
Condescending and ferocious
Pinpoints and executes
Proficiently
The Arctic Fox


# Best Friend's Love
## by Candace Lafferty

He is my best friend
His love for me will never end
He holds me in the moonlight
He always tells me it's all right
That's why he's my best friend
Sometimes friends can be selfish
Others can be so caring and kind
All those dreamy knights in armor
Those are fairytales, men you can't find
So if you read this poem
I hope you will understand
Love's not about the cuteness of the man
It's what's in his heart that counts!


# Hope
## by Christina Fitts

Hope is a twinkling star inside your heart
The last puddle of water on the street
A prayer that you say inside your head
A picture you draw every night at bed
Hope is a bone you must have to stay alive
Hope is the third eye on your forehead to see
And the light at the end of a dark tunnel
Hope is the power to make the clock move faster
Hope is the sun shining brightly to light our paths
Money you find on the sidewalk
And the rainbow after a storm
Hope is today
Hope is tomorrow
Hope is what you live for

# The Cutest Baby In the World
## by Zelika Henry

The cutest baby in the world
Only five months old
He wants to talk and walk
When he meets someone new he puts on the biggest smile you have ever seen
He sleeps all day and plays all night
Sometimes he plays until late at night
My cousin Marcus, the cutest baby in the world


# Dreams
## by Michael D. Barcelos

Dreams are a desire in life
Everyone has dreams in life sooner or later
Dreams can be big or small
Or skinny and tall
Everyone has a dream in life
Dreams can be funny or mean
But everyone has a dream, big or small
Some dreams can be a deep and dark
Some can be good and heavenly
Every one has a dream in life
Dreams can be cute and ugly
Dreams can be immense
And they can be miniscule
Some might be fancy or just plain simple
Everyone has a dream in life
Dreams can be very noisy
Dreams can be as quiet as a mouse
Some can be putrid
And some can be sweet
Everyone has a dream in life

# If I Were Perfect
## by Seda Babroudi

If I were perfect, I would be a goddess
Kind, trustworthy, brave, and modest
The world would bow before my feet
And there would be nobody I couldn't defeat
I'd have A+s all across the board
The world's population would be my disciples, and I'd be their lord
Only if I were perfect, but no, no one's perfect
Not in a world like ours
No superheroes to come save us with their powers
Everyone's full of flaws and guilt
The way the world was supposed to be built
So if the word perfect ever comes to mind
Use a different word of its kind
For nothing is perfect you see
Not even, not even, not even … me

# Cascading Leaves
## by Casey DuLong

Look at the gentle cascading leaves, falling from the tree
Watch as they glide to the glorious earth, filling the children with glee
So colorful they are, just hanging in the tree
The yellow, the red, the orange, so bright, there for the children to see
To see the true beauty of mother earth is something most don't see
But I can see the cascading leaves, just hanging there for me

# Friends
## by Chelsea Cluff

Friends care, friends share
They love the things you do; they will be there for you
As you will be there for them too
Friends care about you when you are ill
They support you in hard times, good times, fun times, and sad times
Friends care, friends share
They say when there is shopping to be done we'll be there
Friends care, friends share, they love the things you do
And when the day is through you just want to say, "Howdy-do, friend"

# Red
### by Jocelin Weiss

Red is the eye from no sleep at all
And the beautiful leaves that return every fall
Red is that itchy, dreaded insect bite
And the poisoned red apple consumed by Snow White
Red is the sky near the restless sea
And the homegrown petunia that cradles a bee
Red is the checker you king on the board
And the blood of the slaves who followed a drinking gourd
Red is the luscious fruit of a tree
And the heart of my mom, who takes care of me


# Love
### by Kyler Pierce

Love is red like rosy red cheeks
It sounds like really mellow music
It tastes like sweet, brand new honey
And it smells of strong perfume
It looks like a big happy smile
It makes you feel happy and loved


# The True Me
### by Haley Mahler

All everyone sees is a beautiful, stunning, fierce, dependable, happy, smiling Haley
But behind the mask I don't really know who I am or who I want to be
Daily now I hide behind a mask concealing my uncertainty of myself
Most of my friends have their own façade of happiness or something
Sometimes I worry they can see through my mask of happiness
But for now I just wake up every morning
And put on this mask without any difficulty
Everyone says, "Oh you're always so happy"
But when they leave me I take my mask off and just be myself, my true real self
I have no self-image, no one to put makeup on for, I just am myself
Everyone should try to take their mask off and try to find themselves
But when everyone leaves I'm all alone, left without light or hope
No one really knows who I am because they have all left me alone and dead

# The Greatest Women
## by Bryan Webb

As we walk and fraternize
She moves like a butterfly
Never knowing where to go
But always holding little Ralphio
Then there's Katherina
Moving through the grass like a ballerina
She is so beautiful
Being such a handful
I, in my orange shirt
Go over and start to flirt
She listens while I talk
And goes along as we walk
She is so nice
I'll buy her anything, even if it is for a ridiculous price


# Blue
## by Andrea James

Blue is sad, very depressed
Sometimes from worry, often from stress
Blue is the ocean, blue is downcast
Utter disappointment makes you blue fast
Blue is the color you turn when you hold your breath
Blue is the color of a policeman's uniform
Blue is what you turn when your heart is torn
When you're blue, you're full of sorrow
When you're blue, you're full of woe
You're even blue when they cancel your favorite show
When I'm blue, I'm very sad
When I'm blue, I feel very sad
Blue is one of my favorite colors
Blue is one of my favorite five
I like dark blue but it is light blue that I despise

# Just For Me
### by Teresa Nguyen

Is he staring?
Is he caring?
That I'm the only girl
That is thinking about him
He's so sweet
Just like a treat
Everyday for me to see
But for once I want him to see
He's the one I want for me
Does he think?
Does he know?
That I'm the only girl he owes
Just one more dance that he cut off
He said, "Go away and buzz off!"
That broke my heart
Into pieces of art
That I tried to put back together
Then I look over and guess what I see
He is slow-dancing a song without me

# Spring Dream
### by Megan Crowley

The sweet scent of flowers dance through the wind
A warm breeze runs its fingers through my hair
A steady fog blocks my view
And suddenly I see snow
My feeling of spring has shattered
And blown away in the icy cold wind

# Purpose
## by Krista White

Who am I?
Who are you?
What are we doing here?
Why were we put on this Earth?
To love, live, and die?
Or to hate, and become immortal
These questions, simple at first glance
Can be as complex as the difference between day and night
Light and dark, good and evil
Or even you and me

# Forever
## by Kiara Dupuy

Forever free, freedom will always be mine
Forever will I be free from the shackles of hate, racism, and slavery
Forever will Dr. King's words be spoken and remembered throughout generations
Forever will we recognize our past to realize our present, and pave our future
Forever, forever will we be one ...

# Things That You Find In the Grocery Store
## by Korena Wright

Eggs, milk and butter
Bananas, strawberries and clutter
Corn, broccoli and potatoes
Celery, apples and tomatoes
Soap, mops and clips
Soda pop, candy and chips
I am sure there is a lot more
In the grocery store

## Untitled
### by Spencer Starzecki

A star inhales every little boy's and girl's dreams
Like they were cries of hope
And then they just fade away like water in a stream
But the moon listens to them and doesn't let them fade away
But holds on to them as if they were his own

## Sky Blue
### by Jacky Man

Sky so blue and true
A never-ending abyss of light and darkness
Always above us in the heavens
Never coming down to say hello
Whining and crying like a baby at times
But always bliss in disguise

## Untitled
### by A.J. Brinkley

A scavenger
Golden brown and dark yellow
Never flies but always soars
Gracefully
The golden eagle

## Let Go
### by Ben Anderson

The flaky blue paint of the dock is brought into focus, as the fog becomes the sea
The shimmering water calls out to you with crispy waves and foamy whitecaps
Freedom is in sight, you picture it in your mind, then you do it
You jump
The two seconds of freedom which separate the warm from cold
Are unforgettable moments
Until you break through the barrier
Into what can only be seen by those who dwell there
And those who let go

# Got a Quarter?
### by Lauren Jaqua

Got a nickel ...
Got a dime ...
Got a ... quarter?
A loner
Stout and focused
Accelerates and adjusts
Quickly
The Quarter horse


# Haiku
### by Moshe Rabinowitz

The Boston Red Sox
World Series champs they are
Go, Boston Red Sox


# Untitled
### by Alex Chaney

Blue shoe
Running in halls
I feel so blue
Living in Parma
Boom!
Deer is dead
Sleeping under the warm sun
Happiness is all around in P-Town
In Parma Idaho
Give a thumbs up
Tick tock sleep
Never wake up

## School
### by Norbert Ordog

Talking to their friends
Till their sentence ends
They blink
Writing papers now
I want to know how
I think
Learning ABC's
Writing with sharpies
Black ink


## Friendship
### by Alyssa Staley

When the threads of friendship weaken
When its flame begins to dim
Another flame begins to flicker
Another thread begins to spin
When apart are pulled two hearts
Separated by a changing world
One small dim candle always will burn
One unbroken thread remain


## Amanda
### by Molly Brown

Amanda my old friend, I miss you so
I wish I could see you; that, I hope you know
Looking at the clouds, I remember how close we were
Looking out your window, petting our toy cats' fur
We were good friends; our bond was strong
When I came over we laughed all night long
We were like sisters; best friends to the end
I hope we see each other someday, my good old friend

# Sports
### by Kellen Ray

Sports are right for me
I love the adrenaline in my veins
My passion, my talent, my time
Every sport I play them all
They're my life

# Family Is
### by Tiffany Slemmer

Family is kind; family is great
Family is helping; family has no hate
Family is encouraging; family is caring
Family is faithful; family is sharing
Family is grateful; family is loving
Family is hopeful; family, there's no shoving
Family is adventurous; family is daring
Family is together; there's no tearing

# A Simple Pleasure
### by Mary Kilcoyne

Have you ever laid down on the sweet smelling, emerald green grass
And took five minutes to watch the clouds dance and play?
If not, I'll tell you the pure magic and fascination
Of watching the delicious coconut snow balls in the sky
To watch the fluffy bunny tails or the delicate angel wings shift
And change in to kitty cats to brilliant ruby red roses
To those little squeaky puffer fish and then to the winged key
That'll open any door if you catch it, it is the most dreamlike part of my day
So the next time you need a break from the too realistic world
Just lie down on the emerald grass and watch da Vinci's
Greatest paintings soar through the sky

# The Statue
## by Tyler Bembenek

The statue sat on the other side of the room
It looked unfinished, but it wasn't
For the work and hardship put into it was full
Making the statue complete
It just sat there in pain and in sorrow, eyes staring out to me
Then it cried out, pleaded for me to help
Pulled me in with its tragedy
Its soul was trapped, trapped forever
Trapped deep within cold stone
Then it hit me, if I was to stay the same as I have always been
With my brain that would not question or ponder
I would stay the same as the statue
Stay trapped forever in agony and unrest
And my soul would never make it out of the stone
The stone to imprison and to depress
And I changed, my brave self came out when it realized that it must
And the new me was complete


# Dreams
## by Kate Donellan

While we're sleeping they come creeping into our minds
Visions of pretty flowers and beautiful butterflies
Or maybe your's turn into reality buildings
Or programs that help the world
Or maybe, just maybe, your little dream starts small
Then grows into a great, big book!
Or maybe just enjoyment comes out of this dream
Either way, big or small, a dream is a dream, no matter how small

# War/Peace
## by Barbara Pacheco

We want peace; we want quietness
The sound of bombs in people's ears
It crashes our dreams
People in the street are poor, being killed and are dying
Do we want that?
Rich people laughing of money, poor people are crying
There is no food on the table
We all see these things, but do we do anything?
War for money, war for oil, war for deaths
People don't get the money or the oil; they only get the deaths
They say God is the reason for no peace
Does he live on Earth?
We are the ones to blame; we are destroying our houses
Peace is all I want
I want to see, feel, hear, touch, and say peace
But I guess for now all I can see, feel, hear, touch, and say is war


# I Remember
## by Erica Cova

I remember the good times, and all the laughs we shared
I remember you and how you always stared
I remember all the smiles you put on my face
And for that, no one can ever take your place
I remember all those hours on the phone
Thinking that I will never be alone
I remember how we used to fight
But your bark was always worse than your bite
I remember how you flirted
And how fast I was deserted
I remember how much you broke my heart
It felt like you literally ripped it apart
I remember how you made me cry
All your love was all just a lie
I remember that dreadful day
The day you broke my heart and went away

## Softball Season
### by Tailor Talbot

Softball comes like a bat being swung
Hitting a ball through the air like we have just won
The pitcher is ready to strike someone out
The batter steps up to the plate, she has no doubt
1st one is a strike, 2nd is a swing
3rd is a hit up the left wing


## Faith, Belief, and Trust In Loyalty To God
### by Dimitri Lamisere

Believe in yourself and you will succeed
Have faith in the Lord and He'll meet your every need
Hold on to your faith; don't ever let it go
Because once it's gone, it's gone you know
Don't be afraid to try
Once you do you'll spread your wings and fly
As high as the sky
Hold on to your faith; don't ever let go
Your faith is your drive
It causes you to strive
When you feel the vibe, I see it in your eyes and hear it in your voice
Hold on to your faith; don't ever let it go


## True Friends
### by Ashley Adelaide Almeida

Staying up the entire night
Getting ready for the pillow fight
Styling our hair for the night out
That's what being a true friend is all about
Taking risks with your friends by your side
Having them there for the whole entire ride
Making sure absolutely nothing will interfere
Especially not those so-called fears

# The American Green Tree Frog
### by Stephen Bessasparis

The tree frog
Slim and rubbery
Springs and leaps
Joyfully
The garden

# Nature
### by Jessica Brockman

Rain beats on the window like a giant humming drum
The waves of the ocean tumble peacefully into silence
The soft wisp of the clouds caress the sky
The clear dew trickles down the huckleberries like a slow moving waterfall
The heavy stones glisten through the peaking summer's sun
The warmth of the sunshine bringing a new day

# Love
### by Daniel Kenner

It lies over mountains and under hills
It hides in valleys and will show itself to everyone
It shows itself to you and you may not realize it
It is watching you
Sometimes you know it and sometimes you don't
Sometimes you see it and sometimes you're blind
It is never blind, it will find you, the wind soars around
The wind soars, as old as time, endlessly like love
Love is immortal, love is invincible
Love cannot be broken, love is pure white
It sounds like angels singing, it tastes like refreshing water
It smells like a rose and feels like bliss
Love is the power of the world

# You Were the World To Me
## by Tyler Cafferty

You were the world to me
You were so much better than TV
I loved you; yes, it's true
But you left me without a clue
Now I'm by myself
Can't ever look at my shelf
Pictures of you and me
Can't believe we were happy


# I Wish
## by Ben Bolshaw

I wish
I was the entire universe
Letting one of my secrets go
One at a time
To all my species
Intelligent or not
I wish
I could soar like an eagle
And see the entire world


# Death
## by Brooklyn Sellers

What is death?
Death is a blackened rose on a windowsill, weathered by the storms
The darkening of leaves, falling in the autumn
The graying of the hair and the weakening of the bones
The end of the end
Gone for eternity, never to return again

## The Spring Days Are Sure To Be Near
### by Rebecca Buffington

"Can you smell the nearby spring?"
"I know that I sure can smell the nearby spring!"
"Do you want to find it?"
"Can't you smell all the flowers come up for air?"
"I know that I can smell them silly flowers!"
"Do you want to find them?"
"Can't you taste the little droplets of dew on the trees?"
"I can!"
"Come and let's count them!"
"Do you like springtime?"
"I know I do because of all the little things that come out to get their first breath!"


## A Stormy Night
### by Mindy Mofford

As dark clouds cover the sky and strings of light fall
As the clouds spread, tears fall from a little girl's fright
Then noise of thunder spreads through human's ears
Winds of high speeds blow the surface as a majestic animal roams around
To try to find the one to bring an end to their story
As the storm's voice of thunder tells the story


## What I Feel When You Are Gone
### by Molly Nettleship

Just for a moment I can feel your lips against my cheek ... but then it is gone
I can smell the fragrance of your aftershave ... then the feeling disappears
I can see you and picture you in my head so easily in my dreams ...
But then the picture just fades away
It feels as if I can touch you ... but then once again, I can no more
At night when I lay in my bed, I can hear you say ... "I love you"
But I know you really are not there
I can once again feel and smell the aroma of your sweet cologne giving me a big hug
But then, it is gone
I can hear you, smell you, feel you ... but none of this is real
I know it is just my imagination
This is what keeps me going every day so I do not break down
Some day soon, this will no longer be an imagination ... but real
-Dedicated to my one and only amazing father, who just came back from Iraq
Charles F. Nettleship IV

## Why Does Love End Up the Same?
### by Talia Pelletier

As the wind blows, I hear a whisper in my ear
I turn around, but no one's there
As I hear my heart beat faster, I confide in the sky
Just look around and wonder why
A chill runs down my spine, water in my eye
Raindrops on my body, empty, broken hearted
Nothing, not a sorry
I've tried so hard to let him go
But somehow my love for him still seems to show
Yet I linger in the rain, trying to forget his name
Why does love end up the same?

## The Earth Is Dead
### by Cory Smith

There is a graveyard next to my house
In that graveyard is a mouse
It will eat you if you cower
It will kill you in the shower
I killed with that mouse
And we blew up a house
We rose up the dead
And they went out and fed
The mouse and me ruled
And the people are all fools
Now the world has finally ended
Because I have descended

## Just Realize
### by Amanda Elisabeth Rogers

Why can't everyone see goodness in every person?
Why can't countries just realize
The peace we could have if we could live together in harmony?
If we had peace in the world think of all the diseases that could be cured
And problems we could solve by working together
Since 9/11 people are not so trusting and willing to work with their fellow man
Because of the hurt and anger everyone feels
As a world we need to come together
And see the goodness in our fellow man and just realize

# Halloween Night
## by Loucinda Herzberg

Feel the tingle in your fingers, feel the rush of fear!
See the streak of lightning ... Halloween is here!
Ghouls and ghosts and goblins up and down the street
While you roam from house to house saying, "Trick or treat"
Feel the stroke of terror from your knee caps to your nose ...
From your shoulders to your earlobes, all the way down to your toes!
As the hand draws nearer to midnight
Mom and Dad say, "Hey, this night's been full of fright!
Time for bed, or you'll be bouncing off the walls
With all that sugar and nonsense and noises in the halls!"
You creep into your bedroom; it's as silent as a tomb
You crawl under your covers when you see a face!
It has an ugly mask and its hair is a disgrace!
It's you, you think with a chuckle, this Halloween stuff has your mind in a muddle
But when you feel your face ... you scream!
You have already taken off your mask, and it is still Halloween!
Mwahaahaa!
The end ... or is it!?

# Gang Wars
## by Lacresha J. Johnson

Seeing my friends die over stupid gang wars
Seeing people fall just cuz of the colors they wore
Seeing my family cry over his dead body
Seeing my homies pour a little liquor on the floor
For the homies that swore they'd never hit the floor
Never seeing my child grow up to have a child
Just cuz she swore she'll never hit the floor
Seeing me run the streets with the colors I wore
Tore my mothers heart, now she's on the floor
All because of those stupid gang wars
I'll never see her smile, never ever any more
Never ever seeing my friends
Never ever seeing my child smile one more time
All because of those stupid gang wars
Now I'm all alone with no one to enjoy
No one to celebrate my wonderful reward
Cuz they had all hit the floor over those stupid gang wars

# Greece, Greece
### by Katelyn Costa

Have you ever heard of Greece?
Where Mount Olympus stands
That's where there is peace
Unless Zeus crushes you with two hands
In Greece trade goes on
And the sea brings them together
They work until dawn
Unless there's bad weather
Only one-fifth of Greece is good for farming
That is where there are green olives and grapes
If there was a different crop it would be alarming
I'm sure glad there aren't any apes
In present day Greece, a peninsula curves south to east
Surrounding Greece are two thousand islands
Ancient Greek settlements were not limited to Greece
And all of the islands have highlands
Greece has many fine harbors
Harbors are places with deep water close to shore
The Greeks probably didn't use barbers
I should be rhyming because this is a real bore
Meat was usually eaten for special times
However, the Greeks found it better to import
Although I'm messing with the time lines
Thanks for your support


# The Sunflower
### by Sarah Gerges

The sunflower with great petals of yellow and gold
It stands tall, showing the backbone of Kansas
Its beauty reflected by the sun's streaming light
It spreads hope and cheer to all
Its pointed petals; its wide base
This flower with a lovely face
Hardy by nature and untouched by cold
It always faces the sun, showing that hope is still there

# The Twinkling Rose
## by Jessica Marie Morris

Best and dearest flower that grows
Perfect both to see and smell
Pink and white of petals light
How your beauty shows and glows
As the day goes and goes
Fold on fold of purest gold
Sweetly scented standing tall
Oh to be that twinkling rose


# The Lion
## by Scott Roberts

The lion
Majestic and graceful
Oversees and commands
Rightfully
The Savannah


# You Told Me
## by Kameko Lindsay

You told me that you loved me; you told me that you cared
You said that you would be here for me and not with that girl over there
You told me all these things but they never came through
So all this time I have been the fool
You told me that you loved me; you told me that you cared
You said you had feelings for me, but not with that girl over there
You told me all these things but they never came through
So all this time you have been playin' me like a fool
So you didn't really love me; so you didn't really care
And you were with that girl over there
All these things, I knew they wouldn't come through
So all this time you treated me like a fool
And if you want to be like that, then we are through

# Dead Love
### by Katie Robb

The cold bites at my skin
Entering, crawling, traveling through my veins
Sweeping through my body like an electric current
Capturing my blood, killing off the oxygen
Closing in on my heart, turning it to evil; it tortures my soul
Struggling in my sleep
Cold sweat running down my panic-stricken face
Trying to stop the heartache
I grasp for something to stop the horror, to stop the pain
My love, locked away behind bars of evil, guarded by demons
Master holds it just out of my reach, taunting me
I realize the only one who can save me is me
And I must learn to love again


# Why?
### by Erin Smith

Why do we stand there and lie
When he hung there to die?
Why do we break commandments
When he hung there to save our sins?


# Fear
### by Nic LaFerriere

Fear is a monster; lurking in the shadows as it watches its prey
Fear is a cloud; enveloping you and those that surround you
Fear is someone out the window
With a dagger drenched in blood from a night's hunt
No flashlight can destroy it; no way to run or hide
It will find you anyway
Run but you can't; squirm if you wish
You'll be just another victim of fear and its cold hand

# Hot Dog
## by Kaitlynn Childers

Furry dogs, small dogs
Big scruffy wet dogs, little muddy brown dogs
Those are just a few!
Nice dogs, mean dogs
Panting-in-the-heat dogs, all different type dogs
Dumb dogs too!
Calm dogs, wild dogs
Don't forget chubby dogs
Last of all, best of all
I like hot dogs!
(I really do like all dogs though)


# To a Daisy I Stepped On
## by Brittney Eklund

You sat in the sun absorbing the rays
Till my foot came down and ended your days
I really am sorry, but you're such a frail plant
I wish I could just fix you up, but I can't
I can take your seeds from you and grow a brand new flower
I just hope my dad will not run over it with the new mower


# The Precious Girl
## by Maxx Tapp

This beautiful girl is like a jewel
Some people mistake her as a fool
This precious girl acts as if she is cool
Her high pitch voice speaks aloud as if she was at school
She strolls past the green trees
And picks up many colorful leaves
Her eyes glisten as bright as yellow bees
Forever she will be precious and always there to please
If you see this beautiful girl, say, "Hi"
Because Precious will be gone in the blink of an eye

## Paper Boat
### by Emily Flynn

Paper boat floats gently
Gets splashed, sinks
And with it goes many dreams
Dreams of success
Paper boat, so vulnerable
Easily destroyed
One wrong turn kills the dream
But still people try
Try for their dreams
And sometimes succeed
Riding their paper boats


## The Aching Soul and Dying Heart
### by Tanisha Rose Lamarre

As I waited for the loud, heartful sounds to stop
I listened to the rain, every water, drop by drop
In one voice, I felt hatred start to rise
Hearing this argument brought tears to my eyes
Then I heard a cry as a loud, dying seal
I ran out of my room and saw an ordeal
She lay on the wooden floor, the texture of mud
Her eyes partly closed, her hair colored from blood
I was very quite scared; she looked like she was asleep
My heart ached from all this madness and soon it got weak
Just thinking about this dark world, no shine, no light
I want to live in a world where the sun can shine bright
No signs of him, no evidence, no clues
The person who killed the one dying at my shoes
I heard footsteps coming toward the door
Soon to think I killed the one lying on the floor
This must hurt, leaving you behind
What hurts even more is this hurt of mine
So this is goodbye, my dearest friend
We will soon meet again when my life comes to an end

# The Soldier In Me
## by Leia Mixon

The soldier in me
My dad said he would never leave
But I never thought I'd see the soldier in me
My dad, he was a drunk
When he'd pass out, my soul sunk
But that's when I became to see the soldier in me
"Why is it me?" I'd say, "Why does it got to be this way?"
But that's when I began to see the soldier in me
But all I could say is that it would be better some day

# Melancholy Lake
## by James Finkbeiner

Melancholy lake
Sits in solemn silence
Peaceful and divine

# America
## by Christy Grimes

America is strong
We keep going on and on
America is tough
But not that rough
We are also fighters
But some of us pull all-nighters
They know us by the U.S.A.
And we will keep on going day by day
Most of us have jobs
But some of the employees are snobs
We try not to get in fights
But some of us act like knights
Well, this poem is almost over
About the beautiful America
Known as the U.S.A.

# The Eradicator
### by Berkley E. Valvero

The tiger
Growling and pouncing
Thrashes and kills
Rudely
An antelope


# Life
### by Jason Courtney

A precious gift, all to treasure
A time to lift, no time to measure
It reminds me of music in so many ways
You don't ever get to pick the rhythm of your days
Life can be rough, like rock and roll
Life can be tough; you may never reach your goal
Live can go smooth, like a love song
You get into the groove; nothing ever goes wrong
Life is there for someone to have or to take
Your life, you can share, or it's a life you can make
Live your life like there's no tomorrow
Full of fun and free of sorrow!


# No Need To Run Away
### by Chantel Butterfield

She always wants to run away
From a world that she does not want to stay
She sits there and wishes away
Until the very next day, when she realizes
That not everything can fly away
'Cause someone once told her
That the only cure is to stand up tall
No matter how many times you fall
And, no matter how many tears
No need to run away from your fears
No matter what happens that day
And no matter what they say
No need to run away

# Thunder
## by Matthew Barnett

Thunder cracks mighty
In the sky. Hit the Earth with
A streak of bright light


# Acid Tears
## by Megan Franco

My tears are like acid dripping slowly down my cheek
For God is the one my heart seeks
My life is getting harder and I don't know why
I hold my tears back and try not to cry
I sometimes think about ending the pain
Then I think, what will I lose, and what will I gain
No one knows how I really feel inside
I put a smile on my face and try to hide
"I know how you feel" is the polite thing to say
But if you don't mean it, take your words away
Tears of acid, tears of pain
So fatal in my heart they leave a stain
I slam my door and jump on my bed
Curled up and crying, wishing I was dead
I smear the acid tears on my face
Praying to God I'll finish the race
I don't often cry cause I try to hide the pain
God is the only one who can keep me sane


# Jace
## by Sarah Buer

Jace is my nephew; he's funny and he's cute
I love him very much and I'm sure he loves me too
He's hyper and he's playful, but he sometimes can be calm
And when I hold his hand, it's no bigger than my palm
When he was a new baby, we made a blanket covered with bears
He still calls it, "My blankie," and he drags it everywhere
Well, now my sister Ali, she's expecting once again
And I hope the new baby's as special to me as Jace has been

## Adversities of Life
### by Chelsea Bacon

Life is a roller coaster
With ups and downs
Twists and turns
Highs and lows
The world flies past you, with your thoughts a blur
And no one gets off until their ride has ended


## Untitled
### by Sarah Woodbridge

I sat in my class
Thinking of any haiku
And, oh, I found one


## I Like the Way You ...
### by Ashley Goodson

I watch your every other move
You just don't know how much I love the way you look
I like the way you walk and talk and much more
I like the way you care about if I take care of myself
I love the way you used to kiss me and hold me
I like the way you care about me
The toughness in your blood
I like the way you have tough love on me
I love, like the way you


## My One True Love
### by Elizabeth Hamlett

I told you I loved you , you knew it was true
Why did you have to be a bama and say, "We're through"
You knew my family, you knew my past
You knew my thoughts, you knew I thought we'd last
When I was scared you felt my fear
When I say I need you, you'd always be here
It didn't seem to last, it wasn't meant to be
When I went to you, you turned away from me
You cheated on me with my best friend
You said you were sorry, it would never happen again

# Ode To Nascar
## by Angelique Harris

The most famous cry in Nascar, "Gentlemen start your engines"
Then say goodbye to all the pigeons
Round and round the track we go, waiting for the green flag to drop
I can't miss a shift or the transmission will stop
As the race progresses we advance through the field
I hope a caution doesn't come out and make us yield
350 laps is all it takes
To finish this race first, will take no mistakes
Too late for dreaming, my spotter is screaming
The caution is out; someone's engine is steaming
The yellow flag flies for oil on the track
After this pit stop I had better get my track position back
On the track, clean up is in full swing
The restart is a comin' be prepared for the whole field to spring
Green, green, green, we're back up to speed; Victory Lane is in sight
I am racing hard and fast, but my car is wicked tight
# 2 Rusty Wallace


# Summertime
## by Avery Hennigar

Hot, humid, sticky air
Summer breezes through my hair
Flip-flops thwacking on hard cement
Blocking sun with umbrellas and tents
Candy melting in my hand
Ice cream falling in the sand
Bathing suits all dripping wet
Cool, icy lemonade, all set
Sandy legs, arms, and toes
Sun block on shoulders and a nose
Tank tops, shorts, skirts, and capris
Painted toes, nails, and bare knees
Insects buzzing at my ear
All the things I love about this time of year
Summertime is my favorite season
It's beautiful and that's my reason

# A Day In Greece
### by Maxine Zeger

One day I walked in the Balkan Peninsula, also known as the country Greece
Barefoot I walked all the mountains, though I did not cut my feet
I got to on a trireme, I thought it was very neat
Next I met all the rowers, but they weren't so quick to greet
Then I ate an average meal which consisted of dried fish
But it was not any good, I would have rather eaten a plastic dish
I was able to make some wine, I smooshed all the grapes
My legs were so sore and achy that I was up very late
The heat was horrendous; I don't know how I survived
The sweat was pouring off me, but that was no surprise
Next I went swimming in a river; it was very twisty and turny
It was extremely hard to swim through, but somehow I survived the journey


# Untitled
### by Devin Robinson

Going for a swim
Take fourteen laps without a breath
Soon you feel weighed down


# When I Am ...
### by Alisha Hassan

When I am a tree, I feel the wind on my branches
The colors of my leaves are orange, yellow, and green
The smell of the roses surround me like a crowd of people
When I am the clouds, I feel like cotton
People think of me when they eat cotton candy or when they play in the snow
When I am a stream, I flow very slow
I run through five different rivers

# Spring
## by Nicholas P. Miera

Spring is finally here
The air is freshly fragrant
Flowers blooming everywhere
Birds are chirping high above, flying free at last
Butterflies flutter their wings, flying here to there
Leaves are sprouting green
Kids playing at the Fair
Ants crawling, eating picnic food
Squirrels waking from winter sleep, searching for seeds and nuts
Amusement parks are in full swing
Pools are ready for the big splash
Vacation plans galore
Spring is finally here


# Somebody Hears Me
## by Byron Hammond

Somebody hears me
On the football team
Oh I listened did you?
Somebody hears me
In the classroom
I did my homework, did you?
Somebody hears me
A group of peers
With open ears, did you?
Somebody hears me
At the church
I listen to the Holy Spirit, did you?
Somebody hears me
Be it good, bad, happy or sad
Did you?

# The Army
### by Caleb Gunn

Red, White, and Blue
These are the colors
Colors that are so true
Fighting for freedom
That is what they do
Going to war as boys
Coming back as men
Capturing Saddam and saving us again
Camouflage uniforms
Fighting through the fiercest storms
The ones that protected you and me
They are the ones that set us free
They are the army!


# Life
### by Breanna L. Irving

I want to talk about life
People are going under the knife
We have a new pope
So we're going to have to cope
The price of gas is so high
It makes some people want to cry
Rappers want all the money and honeys
I think they act like dummies
People are stealing and even killing
They think that they are making a living
Dialing 601
Makes some of us want to call 911
Everyone is trying to fight
At the end everyone is going to see a tunnel of bright light
Life seems so sad
I hope it goes away
Like an old man's hair!

# At Last
## by Lora Dudley

At last it is my time
At last it is time for me to shine; at last it is time
At last it is time for me to be free; at last it is time
At last it is time for us to be we; at last it is time
At last it is time for you to see me; at last it is time
At last it is time for you to be mine; at last it is time
At last it is time for me and you; at last it is time
At last it is time for myself; at last it is time
At last it is time for me to be me


# Flipper
## by Bryonna Pitts

The life
Neither shy nor hesitant
Leaps and squeaks
Joyfully
The bottlenose dolphin


# Each Day
## by Breonna Lowery

Each day I sit to wait for my friends
But no one shows up as the day starts to end
I've sat through each day with a sad broken heart
Someone touches my shoulder, well, that's a start
It was my mean friend who treated me bad
I couldn't help it; I had to get mad
She pushed me aside; it was one of her sick pranks
But I still have friends and for that I have thanks
For I may not have many good friends today
I am making perfect friends each and every day

## The Simple Act
### by Jacey Holliday

Look at the world around you, too many blessings to count
Family, friends, and nature too, add up to a great amount
We take many things for granted, like food and water and beds
But in this life, we have ourselves planted, while other children aren't fed
It is time to take a stand; we should start to face the facts
We can lend a helping hand and give them what they lack
Wouldn't it feel great, if you think about it, you may
Instead of being filled with hate, you could make someone's day
All it takes is a simple act of trying to be caring
It is time to face the facts; for once, do something daring


## Speedy
### by Amber Sterba

An alligator snapping turtle
Lonely but furious
Munches and swims
Never
The speedy


## Silent Secrets of Earth
### by Lee Saunders

A broad incision sits across the evening
The victim to our father's lost war
The restless children sit and mourn the graves
Of those they've never seen before
The lies still an enigma
Still hurting from the stigma
At birth given scars along tender heart liberties
In justice for awkward living situated casualties
My heart bleeding the lonely blood
My cuts filled with dirt and mud
As he picks the deadly knife
On that last day he takes his life
No one cares about his death
The time he took his final breath
Will we be buried among the dead
Remembering the things our friends once said?

## Silly Rabbit
### by Danee' Holmes

Silly Rabbit
Hopping so slow
Green grass under paws
In the backyard
Squeaking
To a cat
The rain starts to pour
The rabbit is so happy!
To go out
Stopped by a hand
The afternoon came and went


## Summer Fun
### by Nadine Durosier

Sun burning hot in my eyes
Usually I can bask in the sun
Maximum of sun to me
My chair and towel used as protection
Excluded, I was, as the sun went down
Reluctant I am

Fun time has to end
Until springtime
Never come back fall


## Contrast
### by Dominic McBrayer

Stand strong against the blows
Of your most fearsome foes
Who remind you of what you have learned
Although, the reason for their cruelty cannot be discerned
They promise and they lie
Wheedle with just enough truth that by and by
You begin to believe them, really you do
And that is exactly when they slide the sword through

## Drugs
### by Shelby Watkins

Look at you smoking weed
Lookin' like a fool at thirteen
Me? I'm fine
No drugs and divine
Don't tell me your secret to getting them
I don't want to know or smoke 'em
You're high, I'm low
You don't know what weed does to you, yo!
You have a sniff, puff, or a whole bundle
I stay at home or go outside and huddle
When you go to the smoke shop and attend to the clerk
He says, "What's up, jerk?"
He said that 'cause you steal from him, tryin' to get high
I just walk by, holdin' my head high
And I look at your face that's lookin' at the sky
Don't do drugs
You'll end up like Chugs
The man in the poem
Who turned into stone


## Grounded
### by Gabriel R. Guzman

I am but a tiny sparrow
A small and meager fowl
Though to the center of my marrow
A prideful bird, I prowl
I come to thee in times of need
For thy unmatched hospitality
But when times come, times of greed
I leave your perch; I must be free
I fly through expanse both high and low
Losing myself in the world around
As I serve myself irresistible fruits
The farther I wander, the harder I am found
A tired creature I come to thee, Master
On welcoming hands I rest my feathers
Clip my wings O' loving One
My round trip flights are done

Bailey McCann

Bailey wrote her winning poem
as an honor student in the seventh grade.
Reserved and conscientious,
she has a deep appreciation for books,
and a great love for animals.
When reading her work,
it is easy to see why
this is not her first creative writing award.

# Autism
## by Bailey McCann

It's horrible to see
When you know you can't help
It's ineffectual to speak
When you know the words are worthless
It is incurable
It's just like being dead - only worse
My brother suffers through so much
Why not me?
He'll never understand why he doesn't fit in
Why the other kids ridicule
Why mom tries to cure him with these things
Like soymilk and fish oil pills
Why he is told he acts two, when he's ten
Why his best friend isn't allowed to play with him
It's like an extraordinary secret
Which he'll never comprehend

Emily Graham

As a new seventh grade student,
Emily divides her time between friends and sports.
She enjoys biking and lacrosse,
and is also a talented pianist.
Reading is still a high priority however,
a pursuit which has obviously helped cultivate
her excellence as a creative writer.

Innocence
by Emily Graham


A little girl
Twisting and turning to music only she can hear
She dances free and wild on the wet sand
As the waves crash and the foam settles
On her little toes
Her arms sway
Her spirit soars
She is alone
But happy
I wish I could be her again

# Division III

# Grades 8-9

## The Beginning of the End
### by Kendall Skelly

Now is the season of fall
Animals hurry
They prepare
Frightening weather
Cold air hovers
Some things die
Can't handle the harshness
Snow falls
And the hardest season will soon come


## In Search of Wonderland
### by Sarah Gibson

Oh, where can my Wonderland be?
Could it be that it is hiding from me?
Should I cry a pool of tears
And ride the gentle waves to the Wonderland pier?
Perhaps the grinning feline could give me a hand
To find that wondrous land
Oh, how I long to see that white rabbit's hopping gait
As he hurries and shouts, "I'm late, I'm late!"
I'd even sit for tea and chat with the Red Queen
And suffer those glares that are oh so mean
To visit a place where babies change to pigs
And cats appear from twigs
Where tea parties are simply quite mad
And the inhabitants are really quite glad
How I wish my looking glass could open the door
So I could visit that place once more
But alas
A mirror cannot be anything but glass
Or can it?

# 911
### by Chase W. Beckstrand

Curse the day when the planes hit the towers
And smoke filled the air like a shower
The people were running in fear for their lives
The husbands hurried and called home to their wives
The terrorists tried to change us all
But America pulled together and rushed to the call
The terrorists were right, our country did change
But in return we worked through our rage
September eleventh was a horrible day
Americans surely went out of their way
To make America a country of peace
It's hard to do when terrorists won't cease
The eagle flies and freedom rings
And there still is a lot of peace to bring
September eleventh is over and done
But will stick in our minds forever to come


# Untitled
### by Shayna Zink

When I come to the end of the road the sun has set for me
I want no rites in a gloom filled room
Why cry for a soul set free?
Miss me a little but not too long and not with your head bowed low
Remember the love that we once shared
Miss me, but let me go
For this is a journey we all must take and each must go alone
It's all a part of God's plan, a step on the road to home
So when you get lonely and cold of heart go to the friends we know
Bury your sorrows in doing good deeds
Miss me, but let me go

# The Fire That Invites Him
### by David Jelley

Standing on the outside, outside all alone, all alone in the cold
The cold surrounds him, captures him, and doesn't let him go
Because he's on the outside and he's looking in, and he sees the fire
Because he is looking and he cannot feel the fire ... he dreams
He dreams while he watches the fire, and the cold wind whistles
The cold that lashes out at him, the cold wind that surrounds him, captures him
The cold wind that doesn't let him go ... the fire that he sees
The fire that he wishes he could feel, the fire that invites him
The invitation he declines; he knows that the fire could not embrace him
No matter how much it touches out to him
The fire, it could not capture him no matter how long it burned
The fire, it could not sustain his life no matter how long he loved it ...


# Tsunami
### by Matthew S. Bishop

Tsunami, a window of drama
Starting in darkness
Gaining
Like the four horsemen
Racing and roiling
Sucking the water out to sea
Growing and growling
Racing like a freight train
Getting faster and faster
Then
Like a sledge hammer it hits
Destroying all in its path
Rolling inland
Sweeping the shore clean
Nothing stands in its way
Nothing can stop it
In all its glory
Suddenly, the water is gone
As quickly as it came
It is gone, racing to
Its next target

## The Soul's Untrustworthy Disguises
### by Alexandra Oderman

I may disguise for you a silent face
So emotionless, yet still questioning
A person who bears not a single trace
Bright with an attitude so long changing
Deep down I tremble in great fear of you
Afraid you will distress me and not love
Loyal to me with no disguise untrue
A clear sight of the hand within the glove
If your friendship remains without my mask
Brought out from within with pure trust and love
An arduous, yet very painful task
A true friend, pure as gold, which shines above
Please my friend let all my disguises stay
Until I love myself another day


## Discovery
### by Josy Wegner

Faraway places
Events gone by
Interesting faces
Make you laugh, make you cry
Cities never visited
Easy to see
Mysteries unsolved
Unraveled for me
In the chair by my bed
Tall mountains I've scaled
In the pages I've read
Seven oceans I've sailed
Stories on pages
Picture it well
Mystical fables
Only books can tell

# My Music
### by Kylie Burgess

The songs of the music box fill my heart with joy
I lie on my bed or in my love sac
And listen to either pop rock or soft soothing sounds that put me to sleep
I love music; I have the very cool extraordinary gift of singing
I have been singing since I was four, memorizing every line
It is comfort, peace, and tranquility all compacted into one
As the voice box vibrates, I move my lips smoothly like the current
Changing range from high to low like a roller coaster
In front of huge crowds or in front of the mirror
Starting out in the school choir, going to county fairs
Then to local clubs, then being a backup singer for a celebrity
To writing my own songs and becoming my own shining star

# Armageddon
### by Dennis Gross, Jr.

I want to see the world of hatred give way
I want to see it all go down
I want tonight to be the last time I need to pray
Because Mother Nature is going to lay everything facedown
I want to see LA get flushed away
I want to see it all go down
I don't want any stops or delays
I want to see it all happen today
I want to watch those hip gangsta wannabes drown
And I will not frown
The world is a three-ring circus sideshow
Where people always fight
And don't know how to talk out problems
I hate this world, ran by problem making people
Who don't know the difference between wrong and right

# Rejection
### by Sean Jackson

It was a cold and dreary day
The rain wept as in sorrow
Almost like it could feel the pain from all those who have lost a loved one
The day grew dark like a soul that has risen from the scorching depths of Hell
This was a day that would truly be like no other
As I looked out to the dark and dreary world
A beautiful rose caught my sight
As I studied its structure and peaceful presence
I noticed the raindrops falling off the petals
Like that of a bleeding heart
A heart that has felt pain for so long
That happiness no longer exists


# Far As the Eye Can See
### by Alexandra Winzeler

Gazed from afar, we watched the spotlight
Wondering what was life like there?
So we struck a plan
We were no one; faces in a crowd
We took on personality
The spotlight made a change
And from this glorious spotlight
Far as the eye can see, people
None of them I knew, and all of them knew me
Things were good on top, waving to fans below
Tossing comments over my shoulder ...
My friends? Where did they all go?
And from this glorious spotlight
Far as the eye could see, people
None of them I knew, and all of them knew me
Standing on the curb at Abbey Road
One last appearance ...
Hiding in our old shadows, to be faces in a crowd
And from this glorious spotlight
Far as the eye can see, people
None of them I knew, and all of them knew me

# The Four Seasons
### by Sabrina Memme

Seasons
Fall, spring, summer, winter
Fall
Leaves slowly changing colors; colors of brown, gold, and red
Brown as dirt after a rainstorm
Gold as a newly shined trumpet
Red as apples picked in October
Spring
"In like a lion, out like a lamb"
Flowers begin to bloom; colors of green, pink, purple, and white
Green as a freshly cut lawn
Pink as tulips beginning to bloom
Purple as lilacs and lavender
White like blooming Easter lilies
Summer
Hot and humid as the desert; colors of aqua and yellow
Aqua like the clear, warm waters of Bermuda
Yellow like the sun, or a cool glass of lemonade
Winter
Cold as an ice cube, trees once barren
Covered with snow as it falls gently and slowly to the ground
Seasons
Year round events
Windy, cool, hot and humid, freezing cold
Amazing experiences and memories


# The Soldiers
### by Cody Brown

Will there ever be an end to this war where we send
Our best troops to fight for what is right
As I sit in my bed thinking of what President Bush said
Pondering on the devastation of Iraq, when will the soldiers be back?
The soldiers will be back when there is peace in Iraq
They now own their land for that is where they will always be able to stand
Some soldiers will not get to see the peace that will be
They gave their own life for a much greater sacrifice
We will win this fight; it will be out of sight!
A celebration there will be, for the soldiers we will see

# Forgotten
### by Kati Petersen

Make no mistake, my hidden heart concealed
I drag myself along the routes of town
My soul is black, a midnight sky revealed
Holding my grief inside for it has drowned
A speckled rock a top a soul island
Lonely and dead, drowning in hopeless tears
Opaque and cold, resting under the sand
Tightened eyes bring forth images of fears
Covered in ash, hidden beneath my shame
Surrounded by seas of weakness and pride
I'm trapped in thoughts, wondering who to blame
Every disturbance kept bottled inside
Who are you, haunted by memory lane
Lost in this world and no one knows my name


# The 25th
### by Daniel Risica

Mistletoe, a big red bow
Time to sew
For the 25th
Action toys, angelic boys
Shop at Roy's
For the 25th
Buying the gift, watching snow drift
Simple smiles give a lift
For the 25th
Christmas cheer, carolers near
Family here
For the 25th
Seeing their face as they unwrap the lace
Don't tell them what's in the case
Save it for
The 25th

## Life
### by Ashley Bullington

People running here and there
Birds flying through the air
The sun is out, people swimming in the ocean
Also tanning on the beach
Kids jumping on their trampolines and running through their sprinklers
But then again there are people dying because of guns or people just being stupid
There are some people getting high but that's just the way life is

## In a Tear Drop
### by Alexandria Paré

Pain, sorrow, death, fear
Loneliness, joy, grace, birth
Glory, laughter, love, hope
Faith, strength, determination
All slide down your cheek
In a tear drop

## Untitled
### by Sara J. Zatir

Dance like no one is looking
Dance like you're alone
It's great to express yourself
When you feel at home
It's really easy to do
Just shake your heart out
With all the feelings inside
Let them pour out
Because it's great to be alive!!!

## Draw Your Last Breath
### by Wendy Walker

Draw your last breath
And join me in death
Like Romeo and Juliet
Together like a silhouette
An immortal love
Traveling as one Dove
Dream the dream of dreams
No more screams
No more waking in the dead of night
All alone with your frights
I'll be there to hold you
As you'll be there to hold me too
Imagine the adventures we will have
When we are together for always, and at last


## A Day of Courage
### by Brady Moore

Two planes hit the Twin Towers, one awful day
Thousands of lives lost and everything in disarray
Firemen, policemen, trying to help those in need
Sacrificed their lives, by doing their good deed
A plane goes down in a Pennsylvania field
Hijackers overtaken by passengers knowing they would be killed
All of these people showed us the courage they had
Even though the ending had made us all very sad
The courage they showed us, and what should be done
I will always remember them on September 11, 2001

## Sonnet
### by Cody Sarle

I love the mountains
It makes me feel like floating on a fountain
I love carving on the peaks
I'm glad you're not weak
When you have snow on your base
It makes me want to ride on the face
All the trees sticking from the ground
Makes me so lucky I have found
You are always there
Standing like the old fashioned hair
People go up there to hoard
But I for one love to snowboard
People look at you as a bad friend
But I don't and we can hopefully mend

## Ruins
### by Kevin Landeen

The day was as dark as night
No light, no joy
The town was empty
Nothing to see, nothing to hear
The silence cuts through you like a million knives
Drawing forth the memories of what was, but is no more

## I Tear My Heart Open
### by Linda Lorraine Hill

I tear my heart open just for you
I love you that much; you just have no clue
If only you knew how I felt
You would see my heart melt
I will be here with you every day
And loving in everyway
I tore my heart open and I found you
I found memories and the things we used to do
I tear my heart open just for you!

# Rain
### by April Manton

Rain is a simple word
Describes the reasons within
I love to hear the sound of the pitter-patter
I gain the sameness of myself
Drifting the time away
I sit on the bench to think about the pain
As rain drips down on my face
I realize I am fed up with this pain
To ask yourself if you're insane
I love it when it rains
I regret to say, that the rain washes away
The pain and tears of a simple day
Rain away to give up the reasons within
Is it such a sin to rain within?


# What Can It Be
### by Janay N. Curtis

It can be crazy
Things may turn hazy
And leave you in a daze
Then things go dark
You try to start a spark
But things still look haze
It can be interesting
And also fascinating
Some people have a lot of money
Think they can buy kids the Easter Bunny
Life can be many things
You don't have to live in Colorado Springs
It can be ...
Rich people with their blinging rings
Think they are big kings
They go to fancy places like Saratoga Springs
And the poor
Have to work to have more
It can be ...

# If I Were In Charge of the World
## by Lillie Scheffey

If I were in charge of the world
I'd cancel all nightmares, bullies, and greed
I'd schedule in happiness, good dreams and good deeds
All of Earth's creatures would live as they pleased
Among all kinds of beings, flowers, and weeds
There'd be cures for the sick and friends for the lonely
Love for the hateful, happiness for the angry
Food for the hungry, thoughts for the thoughtless
Freedom for the captives, a light in the darkness
You wouldn't have hunger and you wouldn't have hate
You wouldn't have anger or people irate
There'd be no pollution because people would care
There'd be clean water, clean bodies, clean air
There would be harmony, love and peace
The fighting would stop, all it takes is elbow grease!
Everyone would treat everything in the right way
They'd keep the hate, and the temper and anger at bay
They'd let love and compassion and kindness run free
We'd all be at peace with the birds, beasts and trees


# Change
## by Christopher Beauregard

Once again, tell me, what was it like?
To watch the leaves fall down
To witness the air getting colder and colder
As the seasons changed
To know the feeling that winter was coming once again
To see the fallen leaves covered with snow
To watch the snow melt
To open the eyes of spring from an icy slumber
To witness the air getting hotter and hotter
Only to get colder once more

# Untitled
### by Ashley Baldo

The hearts of flesh contain
All the true feelings of pain
Sorrow, despair, anguish, and sadness
But also joy, care, compassion, and happiness
So to feel true sadness is to feel true joy


# Love
### by Jerrick Goff

Love can get you in the mist of the night
Love can get you in a sudden fright
Love is a hold on your life
Love has you in a tight vice
Love has a voice that rings out loud
Love has legs that stand so proud
Love is a thing that can't see
Love is a place where you should be
Love is hard work and lots of time
Love is mostly in your mind
Love has the title; it holds the crown
Love can turn that frown upside down
Love can be bitter and also sour
Love hits you at any hour
Love, a word that comes and goes
But few people really know what it means to really love somebody


# Wish
### by Kristin Olsen

In their life they will find something
They will want; they will need, but they will never get it
They will hope; they will dream, but they will never get it
So they will cry; so they will scream, but it won't help
So they will throw; so they will punch, but it won't help
This thing they want is so important
They die
But it was just one little thing
But it was the most important thing to them

# Nothing More
## by Valerie Zamora

I have nothing more than to lose myself in an abyss of tears and sadness
For every tear that has glistened as it ran down my face
And dried with time is proof of how much my heart has ached
I have nothing more than to accept well my defeat and hope for your happiness
I have nothing more than hope for your return
Although I know it to be impossible and this that you said wasn't love
What you now deny; what you now say that never was
It's the sweetest memory of my life
I once had hope in the deepest depths of my soul
That one day you would stay here with me, by my side
And I still kept that illusion that fed my heart
My heart that now can't dream those silly fantasies of our happy ending
And is forced to see you as a friend and even though I lived my life infatuated
And completely wrong, I just don't care because this was love
For my part, the most beautiful, the greatest love
And even though you will forever deny it
To me, it was ...


# Nothing To Live For, Nothing To Lose
## by Andrew Paul Mondry

There's nothing left to lose, nothing left to live for
A blink of an eye and hope is gone; dreams are shattered
What is there to live for now? Love is gone and so is he
Life is long and I am young and there's nothing left to lose
Though he's gone the pain still lingers on
There is too much too soon and so the wall goes up
A brick wall of emotions
So young yet nothing to live for, nothing to lose


# Give Me a Chance
## by Marianne Anglesey

Every time I look at you, I think I have a chance
What chance? You won't give me a chance
A chance to explain why I am the way I am
Why my life is the way it is ... if you'll even listen
Or what I do, or even act around you
You block out everything that has my name on it
Just give a chance to explain

## Empty Road
### by Min Kim

I walk on the road alone
There is no sign of anyone, but just silent trees and me
I have no idea where I'm supposed to go
But I keep walking to search for someone
I look forward and it looks thousands of miles away
The wind is slowly blowing beside me
It's just wind, but my heart is freezing inside
I desperately scream for someone to hear
But only my voice echoes back

## Distant Shore
### by Colt Fridley

Every day I swim an ocean
Fighting your memories like endless waves
Though my river of love flows wide open
It seems like you've dammed it with different paves
One day I'll reach the banks of a distant shore
Where I won't miss you any more

## Dream World
### by Mitchel Howe

My reality isn't the world's reality; reality is absurd
Reality is not, cannot be real
My dreams collide with reality; two worlds are mixing as one
It flirts with that aspect of being as a dream
Dreaming is reality when reality is dreaming
Realizing reality is losing your dreams
Dreaming is reality when you are dreaming
Reality is dreaming when you dream about reality
Realizing the unpassable, unbreakable pass of reality is not realizing your dreams
Dreaming reality is being within a dream
Dream for reality or realize your dream

# Kindness
### by Andy Leiterman

Some people are kind; some are not
Some people help others; some would not
Some people care about others; some could not
Some people are nice; some people are mean
I'll tell you all the kind remarks I have seen
I have heard people say nice things
I have watched somebody get hit
It was so bad, I wished I wouldn't have seen it
I stopped the bad guy that did it
That is the best or kindest thing I have done
I am just happy that the bad guy is gone
He is now in jail for what he did
He should have never hit that poor, innocent kid
If all this didn't happen, I wouldn't mind it
That's why to others, always act your kindest


# How Do I Define Rock?
### by Stephanie Robinson

Marilyn Manson is an ape of god
Kurt Cobain thinks he's dumb
Green Day doesn't want to get a job
Lincoln Park has become so numb
The Ramones wanna be sedated
The Beatles are speaking words of wisdom
Aerosmith was jaded
Foo Fighters are taking things one by one
The Clash will stand by me
Lenny Kravitz wants to fly away
The White Stripes couldn't be held back by a seven nation army
Ozzy's on a crazy train
The Beastie Boys are fighting for their rights
AC/DC is back in black
R.E.M. says everybody hurts
Some people have fury with the Aquabats
These people have rocked our world
With their amazing lyrics
This poem is for them with love
And Moby will always be beautiful

# Dog and Cat
### by Erica N. Wilson

I am a dog; I am a cat
I bark; I meow
I have fur; I have fur
I have brown eyes; I have green eyes
I have toenails; I have claws
I like to play fetch; I like to fight
I eat dog food; I eat cat food
I have a tail that wags; I have a tail that whips
I am goofy; I am mean
I lick your face; I give kisses
I like to run and play; I like to hunt and pounce
I have four paws; I have four paws
I am man's favorite; I am woman's favorite
We are both human's good friends!!

# Forgetful Tree
### by Kevin Lam

Bright golden leaves of memories
Filled with great joy
Flutter to the ground
When winter arrives
Dark clouds of depression form
Dominating the morning sky
Cold winds blow
A falling leaf of twilight stars
Forgotten
A falling leaf of warmth
From the bright blazing sun
Forgotten
A falling leaf of happiness
From a playful child
Forgotten
As the last leaf falls
All is silent
All is forgotten

# Everything
## by Elizabeth Brown

As I sit there, I see her; she, the one who has seen it all
Everything, the hatred, the malnourishment, the mistreatment
Through those green eyes she has seen everything
The death camps, the constant fights against the Nazis
Her 15-year old brother being put to work
Her father being killed because of an escape attempt
It was 1942 when she saw all of this
All the Jews like herself being treated poorly
The ridiculous labors they had to do
The gassings that killed so many
The terror in everybody's eyes
Even today if you look closely you can still see the terror
In her eyes, flickering like an old film
Through the terror you see the millions dead because
Of exhaustion, exposure, and starvation
What you see behind those half-closed eyes is terrible and tragic
And now it is the eleventh of September 2001
The terror attacks have happened, all of the terror is coming back to her
She is frightened, frightened that it is all going to happen again


# Untitled
## by Karlie Rizley

Take me from this place where my "now" seems useless
Every day I fall out of place; everything is useless!
The days go by since I saw you last
I feel as if I could die
I don't want to fade into the past and forever be forgotten
My life turns into years
My dreams turn into nightmares
My life is getting duller and my love turns into tears
I'm now just sitting here thinking of something new
I'm now just lying here dreaming of you

## Winter Has Begun
### by Tom Luchs

Dense white fog is hanging low
Obstructing light from the golden sun
The ground is blanketed in glistening snow
It looks like winter has begun
Gorgeous aspens are leafless and bare
Flowers have wilted, their lives are done
Animals are quiet, sleepy, and scarce
It seems like winter has begun
Outside the air is bitter cold
Sledding and skating in dull, faded sun
Shooting down the icy knoll
It feels like winter has begun
Colorful Christmas lights aglow
Beautiful Christmas songs are sung
Snow covered evergreen needles are shown
It looks like winter has begun
I hear the song of tolling bells
Children laughing, having fun
They watch for Santa's little elves
It sounds like winter has begun
Fires of hope warm our hearts
Joy of living for everyone
A birth of a new year finally starts
It feels like winter has begun


## This Is Just To Say
### by Casey Morrocco

I have broken the window
That was in the garage
And which you were probably hoping
Would keep out the cold
I'm sorry
It was so satisfying
To hear the "Thwack" of the ball against the door

# A Sister's Memory
## by Ashley Swan

What a dear sister she was to me
Her true beauty I could not see
Until she left me drowning in tears
With an absence of love over the years
I remember her face as clear as day
And how her light shown in a wondrous way
I remember her laugh that was so unique
And her beautiful smile that made me weak
I remember the tears that fell from her eyes
Made from all the thoughtless lies
Her voice so profound and surreal
Her damage to my heart no one can heal
But underneath all this pain and sorrow
I still know there is a tomorrow
So with a little hope tucked away in my heart
Whatever the distance we will never part


# Everything Returns
## by Matthew Minahan

The first signs of autumn
Are the apples at the grove bottom
Green when bloomed
Until the red color zooms
So juicy and tart
When it dies, it goes straight to the heart
But autumn will come again
It's like a loyal friend


# Letting Go
## by Mason Littell

Quietly, they drift away, never again to be seen
Their vibrant spirit gone astray to six feet under green
Remembering what they once were like is just that hard to do
You never saw them ride a bike and yet, you somehow knew
You might try to hold on to things, to keep them in, but no
The only feeling that will bring is you have to let them go
That dreaded thought will linger on until you finally do
That dreaded deed that must be done ... I have to do it, too

# My Dark World
## by Emma Springer

I was sad; I was scared; I was alone
I had trapped myself in my own dark world
My own darkness
Then you came through, through the darkness
You were warm; you were safe; you were bright
Light in my dark; one bright light in my dark life
I don't think you know how much light you brought to me
But you left me all alone, alone in my dark
It scares me; it saddens me; I'm so alone
In my own dark world … again
But I'll put a smile on for you and the others
Even though I wish you could see
See through the smile, into my pain, my darkness
I won't cut; I won't do drugs, I won't drink
I won't give up on life; I won't give up on you
My darkness is strong; sometimes it overcomes me
But I won't do those things
Because the dark and the pain are only making me stronger
But I'm still afraid, still sad, still alone, still in the dark
My dark world


# Mean
## by Jennifer Karistianos

People call each other names
Making you feel left out
You have to be like everyone else
Just another clone
Or else you won't fit in
No one cares if you're happy
It makes them happy to see you sad
If you cry, they'll just laugh
Ruining your life
Ruining everything

## Death May Come
### by Zachary Bartlett

Death may come along that could be wrong
It may be a long time before death comes along
Death may come along when you are smoking the bong
It may be when you're in a deep dream
But death will come along even if you're not on the bong
Death will come for you when you least expect it


## Untitled
### by Tiffany Jade Dillard

I used to have a rabbit named Red
He used to live behind the shed
His nose was pink
His fur was as white as snow
He was as playful as a kitten
And as beautiful as a pearl
He was my best friend
The center of my world
How I loved to pet his fur
It's so sad to think that his memory is a blur
He was sweet and kind
I miss him so much
He was like a sibling to me
If there could be such
Now, it feels like he is a million miles away
I miss the days when we would frolic and play
Although you are gone and
I'll never see you again
I just wanted you to know, Red
You'll always be my best friend


## Instead of ...
### by Megan Rice

I think back to when I had a friend that
Comforted me instead of criticized
Made me laugh instead of cry
Talked to me instead of ignored me
Hung out with me instead of ditching me
Always had a shoulder for me to cry on instead of a cold one
And most of all liked me for me instead of my religion

## Yes Or No
### by Sikia Bailey

Do you love me? Yes or no?
You told me once, but I don't know
I told you and it was true
Maybe you are just confused
Are you the one to be there for me?
Or are you there just to break me?
Please don't be the one to do me wrong
Just be the one to stay strong
So do you love me? Yes or no?
You told me once, but I don't know


## When I'm Skating
### by Lexis Alleyne

In winter I go skating
I start spinning and twirling
I'm dancing and jumping
It is so much fun
My brother skates with me sometimes
We skate to music and look so fine
After a while we go to dine
When I go skating, I never think of time


## Feelings
### by Mark Chadbourne

Why is there hate when there is love?
How do they live together?  Coexisting in the same hole called Earth
All of it is so confusing, ready to blow in your face
Caring turns to indifference; love and hate are the same
Feelings cause problems; feelings are problems
If they are problems, why then are they so important to us?
We love, we hate, we care and we don't
Feelings cause war; they also cause marriage and relationships
Feelings
Why?

# Summary

## Summer
### by James William McCune

On a cool, breezy summer day
Young children love to run and play
On the beach, waves crash against the shore
Not even the best surfer can endure
A picnic at the park at quarter past three
I watch a monkey at the zoo swing happily
In the forest up the cliff
Five children get into mischief
An ant colony in the wood
Marching in a line just as they should
On a cool breezy summer day
Young children love to run and play


## Tyler
### by Jocelyn Sellers

I have to let you go, though it's so hard for me
I cared about you so, cause you were my best friend
I thought I loved you but it was just a thought
I thought we'd be together but then you broke my heart
I'm moving on but I won't forget you


## What I Fear Most...
### by Alexis Henry

What I fear most is to give someone my heart
What if they break it and my life tears apart?
Then my life will be off track and after he breaks it there's no turning back
That's why when you say, "I love you" and I say, "No you don't"
It's because I'm afraid in the future you won't
So I guess if you love me, outward and in
This relationship can soon begin
But just one more test to see if your love is true
Prove to me that always, love me you'll do

# Aging and Onions
## by Cortney Maples

Aging is like an onion because of many reasons
Just like us humans, onions develop through the seasons
"Onions have layers," said the great green shrek
Both onions and aging can seem like such a trek
Each layer telling of one's self
Telling a story like a book on a shelf
Getting older and cutting an onion can make you cry
Like some say, "It's better to be wet than dry"
No matter what happens we'll still be the same
An onion is still an onion and there is no one to blame


# Looking To the Velvet Sky
## by Nicholas Worley

The piercing of my inanimate skin is a time of solace
The pale blue moon shines brightly, bragging its eloquence
On the lichen-covered hill, I sit in deep reverie
Sinking into the past, present, and future
I am suddenly submerged in tainted brackish water
Although I am desiccated, the water doesn't become potable
I beg, I plead, I scream to the water
If only I could take a cusp to the white caps of the waves
Now suddenly, I am lying on the sand
I look above and feel the forever-welcomed embrace of the giant lemon in the sky
My ears are filled with an annoying, yet somehow soothing sound
The gulls sing to me, speaking in an unknown tongue
That not even a polyglot can comprehend
They glide aimlessly, trying to find nourishment that cannot be found
Suddenly, the blue of the sky is painted black and shrouded by stars
The effulgent stars transcend on to my body, tickling me, like fish in a brook
The sensation was the trickling of my essence, escaping me to find a safe haven
Into the velvet sky I ascend watching the monolithic statues fall defying him
I enter a beautiful place where I am adorned
With beautiful garments and flowers of undiscovered hues
I now watch my world fall into the depths of an endless abyss
It wasn't really my world anyway
Just a waiting room full of misfortune and corruption

## A Poem's Value
### by Samantha Casey

Written poems fade with time
Most half read then published for a measly dime
Hopeful words and shattered dreams
Many a poem goes unseen
Thoughts and emotions free and running
Beautiful words gathered in summoning
Read with understanding and grace
Poems cannot be a disgrace
To the author their poem is gold
Such hard work shouldn't go untold
However, the world takes quick gazes
And sees many a mind-boggling word mazes
To the ones who just want meaning
Can go on looking and steaming
They'll never be able to recognize
A poem's true meaning because it's in disguise
But when all the picking and prying has been done and said
Here lies a poem's value forgotten and dead

## Greatness
### by Caitlin Davis

In greatness there lies a fire inside
True passion that ignites the soul within
Sweet tolerant heart emblazoned with pride
A spirit soaring free from sordid sin
Appreciate simple pleasures in truth
Gratefulness sanctifies the splendid mind
Pure as a child dawning on sacred youth
Thriving on knowledge both simple and kind
Leadership shows how a great one is strong
Testing the limits like the great ones before
To stand, for the people cannot be wrong
A powerful leader forever more
Powerful thoughts are an honor of life
Returning to haunt us, as signs of strife

# My Eraser
## by Zachary Rotz

My eraser is pink
So is my kitchen sink
I do like watching The Weakest Link
But it does make me think
So I just get up and help myself to a drink


# The Way a Poet Knows It
## by Deirdre Judge

It seems only a poet knows
The way a story really goes
And so I tell of stormy nights
Filled with wonder, thrill, and fright
I project the image of protection
From the warmth of friends' affection
Visualizing memories long past
Hoping that these pictures last
I paint buffets of luscious pastries
Mighty high and sure to be tasty
I recount gorgeous autumn days
Rainbow trees and skies of gray
Summer nights and what I show
The sky so dark, the moon aglow
Dew settling on the petal of a rose
A puppy chewing a garden hose
I tell of stomachs full of butterflies
When young girls meet young guys
I show death and deep depression
And true teenage aggression
I expose backstabbers and those who lie
And how all they do is make you cry
The world's dilemma is what I preach
While peace on earth I try to teach
I write of war and fighting
That hits unexpectedly like lightning
I supply a refuge for those in stress
For in another's shoes they can dress
And forget about their worries
They'll feel better in a hurry
And so I write for everyone
For I cannot stop once I've begun

# Ex-Wonderful
## by Lyndsay Simon

She had never felt true love before
Her teenage heartbreak from her boyfriend running out the door
Her soul has never felt so sore
They all say things but no one really knew what they had
It started out so good, but it turned out so bad
They try to talk to her but they know she is shattered inside
Her idea of reality in her mind is fried
There was such jealousy of this beautiful romance
He was the only one who gave her a chance
No pretty love songs or happy laughter
And she can't let herself live happily ever after


# Nowhere Man
## by William Reid Franke

I'm a nowhere man setting in a nowhere land
Waiting on the one to bring me to somewhere where I belong
The one I'm waiting on is a blonde
She has the most godliness hair, the best ruby red lips I have seen
And her eyes starrier than the midnight sky
I am just a nowhere man setting in a nowhere land
Waiting on the one that was made for me
To bring me from this darkness of loneliness and despair
I just wait on her to release me from this darkness I have created


# Who I Am Today
## by Christina Wiech

Every morning when I wake up, I do not think about who I will be today
For I'm too busy bustling around the house
Trying to get ready to be a person I know I am not
Trying to live up to the person you want me to be
Not being the person I know that I am
And when I finally get to my school and see all the faces that are really masks
Just a way to hide who you are
I decide to take mine off today, so I can see what will happen
When the feelings inside are released
And if you decide to laugh at what I say or what I do, it won't mater to me
For today I have taken off my mask

## Sorrow
### by Andy Ulmer

The Lament passes my ears
Heart jumps, skips a beat
Hear and follow it, contemplating
Stately raven perched in a tree
Full of the gloomy dark rain
Staring baby tumbling from nest
Mother, with mangled feathers, drooping eyes
Chipped beak, tail feathers awry
It flits, ensnared by old leafless tree
With quick high paced, gloom filled song
Until the dark hours set
Teardrops fall from the dewdrop eyes
She fell heart broken


## Untitled
### by Ali Grzywna

A cricket's trapeze
Glorious bitter mornings
With autumn's orchestra of wind
A sun-whisked breeze
Rocking chair symphonies
And cheerful puddles of the violin
In summer's ease
A vibrantly drab, cold gray
Sunset compared to
Macaroni and cheese
A field of dandelion and crown of clover
Across to moon-shined freeze


## Lonely
### by Lindsey Kaye Elliott

Look out the window, the car driving away
Never does she realize, Mom isn't coming back
House cold, so quiet; can hear a pin drop
Every night she lies awake, crying, feeling nothing
Teardrop after teardrop fall from her face, feel never ending
A puddle formed on her pillow growing with time
Day turned to night, but sorrow and despair remain

# Nature
### by Vincent Serrazina

The trees are blossoming
The birds are singing
Children outside playing in the sweet, sweet air
The birds sing such beautiful songs
The trees now are blossoming and they make a place for the birds to stay
When the children get tired of playing, the trees give them shade
So they can rest and get away from the hot sun
In nature, everything helps one another survive in this world

# Escape From Slavery
### by Talia Kemp

Wandering the forbidden streets at night
My loved ones and I are filled with fright
Searching the houses for the sign we know
Where there lives a caring family to show
There hangs a quilt swaying in the breeze
My family and I fall grateful to our knees
One step closer to the end of our trip
Never again will we hear the crack of a whip

# World Peace
### by Thomas Aguirre

When soldiers have to go to war
They just can't stand to watch all the gore!
It's very painful for them to see their friends die
All they would do is just cry, cry, and cry!
"What do they want?" they may ask
World peace; that's their task
They want it 'cause they don't want to go to war
They just can't stand fighting anymore
As for me I want world peace too
As much as I want the sky to stay forever blue
But for soldiers, people, and you
World peace would be, a dream come true!

# Cheerleading
## by Danielle O'Neil

I'm an awesome flyer, I go so high
I go so high; I almost touch the sky
I can go on one leg
My base's name is Meg
They throw me up, up
We call it a pop
My uniform is black, blue, and tight
I have to use almost all my might
We all have to be together
And I'm as light as a feather


# Lebron James
## by Joshua C. Butterworth

The man named James
The best of the best
No one is the same
The man named James
He knows how to play the game
He never needs a rest
The man named James
The best of the best


# The Days To Remember
## by David Robb

You wish this moment would last
But it will always be a memory from the past
You wish that you wouldn't have to go
But at the same time you want to
The unsure feeling of happy and sad
Now's the time to remember all the great things you had
Walking home from school
Swimming in the pool
The days you cherish so much
The times you want back just once
So then you leave; you're on your own
Wishing to go back, but no one is home

# Goodbye
## by Ashley N. Taylor

My final confession was hard; I didn't understand what I was saying
I thought I could go through it, but I couldn't
Many people tell me to be strong and be the person you always are
But I didn't know who that person was
It takes some time to really know who I really am
Everyday I try and I'd try and try
Knowing that someone loves you can be terrifying
Because you don't know if you should love them back
I never had trouble trusting people until it got personal; then it all changed
I knew I had to move on but I didn't know how
I kept trying, but it never worked; I guess I wasn't trying hard enough
I thought I could, because once the pain is there you want to let it go
I did once but it came back to haunt me
I've been pressured and hurt; knowing that brings everything back
Once I found him I thought he was the one, but no one is the one; never
I don't believe in the one, the only one
It's just a powerless saying people want to find in their lives
I miss you but I don't at the same time and I don't know if I should
He made me laugh and made me smile, but now all he does is make me stronger
I learned a lesson from all of this; to know I'm better off with or without
I found out the truth and I was devastated
And all I could think about love was that it is despicable
And that's all I got to say; goodbye to the past
Goodbye ...


# One Chance
## by Craig Sacra

Walking onto the baseball field, not knowing what I got myself into
I'm not sure what might happen in this game
Will I make the winning hit, or will I make and error and sit?
Only one thing goes through my mind when I'm on the field
Is someone watching?
My dad always says, "Play like a scout is in the stands"
I do; I tell myself that I am going to make it into the major leagues
No one thinks I will though
You only have one chance to prove yourself worthy
To me, I think I'll take that chance and do something good with it

## Treasure Time
### by Kelsey O'Shea

If life is fleeting fast then let us play
Live the way you want to live, be a star
The years go by, the times will fly, each day
So live like it is your best day by far
Do not go hide when you should cry, be brave
Realize your goal, be true to all, don't fray
Say what you think, don't take it to the grave
Cherish your opinion and seize the day
Don't be afraid to take a risk, and rest
Do what you feel, act how you want, not shy
Be all that you can be and do your best
Be who you are, do what you can to try
So take a chance, and if you fail don't stop
If you succeed you are on to the top


## Snow
### by Corrin Rausch

The newly fallen snow
Lays like a quilt
I cannot help stepping outside
To feel the downy flakes
Although my toes are frozen
I stay outside to gaze
At all the falling snow
All is quiet
I finally go back inside
And look out the window
A hint of light glistens
On the blanket of white
The world looks so perfect
Wrapped in the peaceful winter

## How Things Change
### by Pamela Keilig

For several months I saw you as someone I could trust
Many minutes spent giving you the best advice I could
So why is it now, avoiding me is a must?
Now it's clear you have a heart made of wood
Your reasons sound like pathetic excuses
All the memories of days not too long ago
Rearranging themselves in my mind, there is no use
To holding these feelings that you let go
Who knows for sure what you're really thinking
Maybe you don't even know yourself
But still, when you are near my heart is sinking
Clever boy, too bad lying isn't good for your health
Don't even ask me why I hope
When obviously you're incapable to cope


## Why Bullying?
### by Kaitlin Patricia Happnie

Bullying
Sad and cruel
Not necessary
Mean not fun
Bullying
Why?
Why do they do it
Being mean to other people ...
Why?
It's cruel, not fun, not amusing
Why bullying?


## Alone In the Dark
### by Laura Neu

You made me feel alone in the dark
The day you gave me a big black mark
You held me tight, then you threw me away
My life is dark, it never seems like day
The mark you left is full of pain
My laughs and smiles have all drifted away
You ruined my life when you left the mark
And now I'll forever be alone in the dark

# The Abyss
## by Alex Jones

Hopes and dreams are overrated
All my smiles were confiscated
Never was I told
What the future would hold
I'm drowning in innocence
The words flowing from your mouth make no sense
In your sleep you cry the blackest tears
Your dreams are haunted by your deepest darkest fears
Images of what life has in store for you
Hoping, wishing, praying that it's not true
Pictures of such pain and sorrow
Is this what I live for?  Is this tomorrow?
I fight this never-ending battle
In the made up world in my mind
Where your demons are what rule
And love and reason are blind


# Fall Vs. Spring
## by Brian Tougias

The colors are green and gold
The leaves are very bold
In spring there is much delight
The scenery is so bright
In fall the leaves are orange, yellow, and brown
Nobody really gets down


# They Bruised His Soul
## by Nadia Mahmoud

They called him names
They called him names
They taunted him and bruised his soul
Nobody, but him knows how much it hurts to be told the things he was told
What they said
Constantly ran through his head
Even when he tried to sleep
The names he was called kept running through his head
He even tried to count sheep
But he always cried himself to sleep

# Crystal Snow
### by Kathleen Doherty

Sitting in class
Staring through the glass
Out at the freshly fallen snow
Waiting for time to pass
To when I could be where the wind will blow
I see the piles of crystal snow
But for now, I am stuck where I am supposed to be
And that is all I know

# Black Hole
### by Karisa Lyn Smith

Have you ever seen a black hole?
I have … well, this black hole is a backpack
A teenage backpack is full of overdue homework and yesterday's egg sandwich
This black hole smells of dead things and wet dogs
I've found something I didn't want to find
In the black holes of ours you never know what you may find
My teacher says we need to clean these black holes of ours
We all reply in a cry, but we don't know what we will find
So I say to you, clean your black holes A.K.A. your back pack

# Wishes
### by Traci J. Lenny

Why do people wish on stars or throw a coin in a fountain?
Do they desire more to life?
Maybe that special person
That one who will always be there during your worst times
When it feels like no one else cares
When nothing you do matters
That someone who was there from the start, but you never knew they were there
Until that day you felt like dying, but they turned that all around
All of this may sound nice, but remember it's only a wish

# Soccer
## by Tori Conlon

The players wait around a white semi-circle
While tension builds like a volcano waiting to erupt
And then the whistle blows
Like the shrill calling of a seagull
On a coastal summer's day
The ball that has been sitting in the circle
Is now sent across the grassy field
By a strong kick of the multi-colored opponent
And the players run after that black and white sphere
A cleated foot juts out to try and get the ball
Once in control, the player tries to run as fast as the wind blows
Past the opponent the player sprints; the defense tries to oppose
Too smart is she; she runs right past and the goal gets bigger by the second
The goalie is on her toes waiting, sweat, dripping down her face
Here comes the forward with the ball that screams
"Kick me now, here is your chance!"
The forward lets out a swift kick
A powerful kick that sends the ball through the air
The goalie pounces like a lion on its prey
But to no avail, the ball lands nimbly into the net

# Wind
## by Sarah Sharp

In my backyard
I listen
For wind's song
Chimes
Whistle
How magical
Just as it comes
To a halt
I yearn for it to come again

## Snow Day
### by Nicole Conti

The kids are calling
The snow is falling
Outside it's really cool
There is no school
Kids are making snow forts
And snowmen of all different sorts
Because of the snow
The kids glow

## Sunshine
### by Nandinii Novoa

Sunshine responds to the call of the Earth
The beginning of a beautiful day
Like a baby's first smile
Sunshine is happiness and
Warmth to flowers
Stopping and crying of a sad person
Filling our days with love

## The War of the Sandbox
### by Tucker Weatherly

The sweat pours from his glands like water
He runs to his convoy to avoid being slaughtered
With the metal shield being his only friend
He can hear death coming to make amends
Now he leads a group to a nearby building
They are all hurt, but are still willing
To fight for their friends and family back home
And for all the months they've felt alone
The soldiers gather together for a final push
Their last chance lays on this ambush
The man loads his gun and kisses his favorite picture
With the sand and blood, it makes a terrible mixture
So they all yell and run to their enemy
All the shots are fired without a scent of serenity
The strategy worked; only two men were down
One was the father with his daughter's photo on the ground

# Football
## by Ian Amor

Speedy offense
Chases a pig across a dirt plain
As bright coaches
Run their mouths madly
Concession cashiers
Sweat themselves dry
While a strong defense
Dives for the hog

# A Baseball Field
## by Blake Jolly

A baseball field
Where dreams are made
So happily heaven smiles
While people laugh and play
Unless you get hurt
Then they fade
Just like the shade of each day
Running for baseballs in the sky
Makes you feel like you can fly
Ground balls screaming at you so swift
Will make it feel like a very fast gift
The ball coming at the plate so fast
Then leaving the bat like a blast
People yelling in the stand
The voice of a million soldiers in a band
The food they have feeds the soul
From inside it makes you whole
The umpires screaming so loud
Will sometimes make the crowd very unproud
Thousands of players have played this game
And they all had their spot of game
A baseball field, is a field of dreams
The kids' dream, to play for their favorite team

## Untitled
### by Josh Moriarty

A hat in the waves
Floating right on by
Over the ocean caves
A hat in the waves
It floats there gently as the ocean behaves
The hat floats there, who knows why
A hat in the waves
Floating right on by


## A Never-Ending Circle
### by Lacie Tidwell

A never-ending circle
Circle of life, circle of death, circle of popularity
A circle of outcasts, a circle of jocks, a circle of nerds, a circle of me
A group of circles and one all alone
Everyone has a group, everyone but me
An outcast, a soloist, a psycho, a loser
Cheerleaders, football players, skaters, and me
I am all alone, alone to travel, to look out for myself, to live


## In the Dark
### by Kelsey Elizabeth Davis

Anything can seem scary
When the lights are all turned off
And you're left all alone in the dark
Like the misery of the moaning and groaning ghost
That is only the howling wind
Or the menacing, snatching hand
That is just the tree branch hanging in front of your window
Frightening images appear in the darkness of your bedroom
And vanish just as soon as the sun's morning rays stream in through your window
Like that exquisite, porcelain doll
Whose head twists all the way around
And whose eyes bore into yours when you turn towards her
But these bone-chilling notions seem ridiculous once the sun's shining
Still, when those lights are no longer on
And your possessions seem to come alive
Everything can seem scary
When you're in the dark

# This Chubby Golden Man
## by Matthew Cipollone

The land became wet like the ocean with skies as dark as my basement
For a gray man passed making things this way, but he won't return
Instead he ran, frightened by my brave soul
I would have chased after but he left me a friend to play with
This chubby golden man
A wonderful and bright wardrobe if I do say so myself
People tell me his name is Sonny
One thing is for sure, he's very beautiful
Everyone thinks Sonny is amazing
By the way people talk about him, it seems he gives everyone the energy to live
He probably thinks that the world revolves around him

# The Doors
## by Sam Brown

White and tall and double sided
With hinges painted white but will never turn
The runners cannot be found because they want to hide
White like the clouds, not green like the fern
The doors are solid with thick insides
They stand beside the wall's side

# A Golden Morning
## by Luiza Rapoport

I heard it dwells from every mountaintop
A bright sensation lighting the black night
The golden sunshine it will never drop
It covers the darkness with broad daylight
And yet it comes, a soothing ocean breeze
The night is fading into a new day
It rises swiftly from the ruffled trees
You hear the children going out to play
They call it morning from what I have heard
Listen real closely as the morning comes
The glorious whistling of a bird
And the lyrical beating of the drums
It wakes at sunrise and then it must go
But why it comes, one can never quite know

# The Sun
### by Mallory O'Connor

People lay out just for you, to feel your warmth and light
The bright color and neon personality
People study you, to try and figure out your randomness and brilliance
People pay big money to try and replicate you
Ladies will kill to get the golden color you give
The plants and the flowers adore you
And none of us would be here if it wasn't for you
But yet there's the unexplainable
Like why something so useful and reliable can be so dangerous
You cause burns and cancer and lead to people's death
Know that people still couldn't do without you
And knowing that people still love you!


# I Am
### by Jessica Sentilles

I am a godly girl in an outgoing world
I wonder why people don't believe
I hear the struggles people are going through
I see their sadness shine through
I want people to have faith in God
I am a godly girl in an outgoing world
I pretend that the whole world believes in God
I feel the presence of God flow through me
I touch God's heart as I praise Him
I worry that I won't be able to do His good deeds
I cry when others are hurting, and I can't pull through to help
I am a godly girl in an outgoing world
I understand that I can't help all, but I keep on trying
I say, "God is with you and is calling you to believe and trust"
I dream of this outgoing world being more humble to God
I try to follow in the lighted path
I hope this world will become a better place
I am a godly girl in an outgoing world

## Coming This Fall
### by Andrew Moulton

Fresh new series in the fall
Ends in summer, time to call
Your friends when the one they missed
Is replaying, they must tape it
Seasons go on, they're all the same
Actors on it lose their fame
Seeing it doesn't matter now
The show gets cancelled somehow

## Future
### by Karen Urban

What does the future hold for me?
Happiness, sadness, or even glee?
The wind will blow me the way I need to go
Which will guide me with a stern hand
What does the future hold?
This is what I've been told
The future is a horrible place
An absolutely terrible place
And this is what I say
It's only like that, if you make it that way

## W.W.W.
### by Kelli Enyeart

She's really not so nice and the kids say she's made of mice
With just one look into her piercing red eyes she can make a grown man cry
She has a green pimple covered face with a long greasy nose and sharp pointy ears
A wiggle of her ears and poof! You're a frog
Most adults simply say she doesn't exist
No creature could be that hideous
But the kids still believe she's out there
For she is the Wicked Witch of the West

# Hearts of Hearts
## by Laurie Polderman

To love, and to be loved, owe respect and give love
To have a heart full of love and let it flow freely
But instead you have given respect and are in debt of love
To keep inside and to be in a jail, I have let go and I was given peace
You aggravate and I keep my cool, if and when I lose it; I am raging with anger
I become a reckless fury
I cry, but you don't see
I get lost at sea and you don't care
Suddenly, I see the light
My friend, my dear, dear friend, I see that you care
You have found that my heart is broken
You attempt to heal me with your everlasting kindness
You call upon my name and it's good to know that I've got a friend
In this cold, cold world of heartless people
You've kept me up when I've been falling down
Since you do this for me, I do the same for you
I protect you and you protect me, I owe you my life
I don't deserve you as my friend, I am glad for you
He holds you tight
He sees the sparkle in your eyes that you have for him
And he holds the same for you, I love you
You are my friend and the very best of
I am happy for you; the one I loved didn't love me as much as I loved him
I was hurt; he took me for granted
I fell in love over and over with you, every time that I have seen you
I have never felt this way
You gave me pleasure, but so much pain
This is not how love goes
If you love or loved me
You would be out of your mind over losing someone like me
You would be doing anything to win me back
You still talk to me, but that is not enough
You should have done this and you should have done that
Now would be a good time to change but it is a little too late
I had the times and moments of my life that are irreplaceable
Some of them I owe to you, you took my breath away
But now it's all over and my heart has forgotten you

## Spiritual Dove
### by Ashly Wright

Once there was a girl, whose parents died long ago
So this is how the story goes
I met her on a foggy night
In the bitter cold, as the moon shone bright
She told me of a sad-less love
Much like an eagle or a helpless dove
She said that she could only blame herself
But, I myself, blamed everyone else
For as I look back, I should have guessed
She would get hurt, just like the rest
For she was black, and I was white
The whole world saw us as a hideous sight
But we just held our heads up high
As the whole world seemed to pass us by
She was killed before my eyes
And all I could do was hold her and cry
She told me that she finally had a someone to love
And when she died, remember her as a dove
There's no one in this world I could ever love
Only my daughter, the spiritual dove

## An Only Child Is Me
### by McKenzie Hicks

My name is Sally, I am but only three
I am an only child; guess it was meant to be
My parents buy me stuff, from stores and magazines
I've seen London, I've seen France. Hey, you have to have these things!
I always get my wish, and never have to lose
And when I throw a tantrum, they take me on a cruise
My tummy's full of sushi, and my room's full of gadgets
Of course they only love me, not he or she, just me, me, me!
My parents wake me up, each morning at ten o'clock
Even though I wake up late, I never go to bed at eight
I always watch TV, with my but' ox on the couch
My mouth is always busy, chewing things all about
My room's a big mess, with clothes on the floor
There's so much inside here, I'd say it's a store!
I am spoiled you see, and I know that is true
I don't really care though, because I am not you
My name is Sally, I am but only three
You've seen how my life is, please don't bother me

# Cliques
## by James Carlson

Where do I fit in? I have no clue
Am I a jock that needs new shoes?
Am I a geek that gets stuffed in my locker?
Or am I a guitarist that sees myself as a rocker?
Am I a gothic that dresses in black?
Or am I a nerd with pens and a tack?
Am I in the smart group, always getting an A?
Or am I a teacher's pet, always getting my way?
Am I in the popular group, who everyone wants to be?
Nah, I'm just me


# Death
## by Jacy Zimmerman

What if you woke up and no one else was there?
Would you cry, would you panic, or would you be frightened and scared?
If the person you loved most died this very day
Could you continue on?  What would you do?  What would you say?
Well death isn't something that you can just change
So live life to the fullest each and every day
Let people know you love them even if they don't have a clue
Because someday they'll be gone; who knows, next could be you


# Fly High
## by Julia Vinson

My spirit is lifting me higher and higher
My body is growing lighter and lighter
What little strength, my body once held, is growing and growing
So much so that my heart is exploding
Off I go, and I won't ask why
It is all up from here; I am going to fly
Through the trees and up the mountains, till I have reached the sky
I won't give up; I can do this, all I need is one try
Before I knew it, I was done and I feel so great inside
I know I'll do this again very soon, so to the ground I glide
It is your turn, to journey to the sky
Don't let anything pull you down and you too will fly high

# Love
### by Charly Elizabeth Johnston

Love is a token
It shall never be broken
We tumbled into each other's lives
We should grow older and share special times
Love is a token
It shall never be broken
We quarrel over ridiculous things
But in the end we both have rings
Love is a token
It shall never be broken
Let's live our lives together
Forever

# My Bubble
### by Francina Huggins

I live in my own little world and only ever touch the edges of the worlds of others
I am sometimes welcome, pulled into their world, and out of my bubble
Sometimes I am unwanted, and stay on my side of the line
Most of the time, I am content to just stay in my world
And not try the boundaries of others
Occasionally, I want to break free
Daringly cross the fence that holds me in, but not often
Inside my bubble there is no feeling
Outside there is joy and pain, happiness and loss
I try not to venture out of my protective shield, but sometimes, I have no choice

# Overload
### by Marianne Meads

My head aches, oh, how it aches
The black and white Xerox paper races through my mind
Oh, how my head aches
The papers, the many, many papers
Papers from math, papers from science, papers from history
Oh, the piles and piles of papers
The tests, the many, many tests
History test on Tuesday, science test on Wednesday, make-up test on Thursday
Overload, overload, my brain can't hold anymore
Oh, how my head aches

# Do You Love Me?
## by Jennifer Brogdon

Do you love me or do you not?
You told me once, but I forgot
Do you even care about me?
Are you going to be the one who is proposing to me on one knee?
Are you going to take care of me?
Are you going to be my one and only?
Are you my number one, my superstar, my mate, my life?
Or are you just going to turn around and stab me with a knife?
Will we stay up talking on the phone all night?
Will you be the one I call to make sure that everything is alright?
You're the only one I ever think about
I hope you feel the same way about me, because I have not one doubt
Will you ever break my heart?
I hope not, but if you do my life will be torn apart
So the question is simple
Do you love me or do you not?
You told me once, but I forgot


# It's Springtime Again
## by Kathryne Wagner

Early in the morn
Frozen crystals rest on buds
It's springtime again
Sun illuminates
Trees awake from a deep sleep
It's springtime again
New offspring are born
Baby deer and birds emerge
It's springtime again
Sunlight pours softly
Damp grass and petals shimmer
It's springtime again
Roses deep color
Everything is new and calm
It's springtime again

# Poetry
## by Terri Henderson

Poetry is a way to express your feelings
Poetry is my favorite pastime
Poetry is almost like a song, sung to the birds
Poetry is like dancing outside on the brightly colored grass
Poetry is a relaxing thing to do when you are tense
Poetry is like water running from the faucet
Instead of water, what is running from the faucet are poetic words
Poetry is a flow of words all lining up, forming a picture to see
Poetry is a talent that many can have
Poetry is something that comes to you; it is your inspiration
Poetry can inspire others to take on the role they were put on earth to take
Poetry is a sudden flow of words being put together to make a certain meaning
Poetry is in you; it can lead you, and change you
Poetry is like wind blowing through the trees
But poetry blows through the pages of a book
Poetry is like a beautiful woman; poetry is the body of the title
The title expresses what the poem is all about
Poetry is like a shining star in the sky
Certain poetry shines out more than others
Poetry: it is soothing, like a relaxing bath
Poetry comes to you and then it can leave you
Poetry comes in different forms; it is like colors
Poetry showers you with words that cleanse your mind
Heal your soul, and calm the heart
Poetry is like a medicine waiting to cure your sickness
Poetry can open up your heart to something new and unusual
Poetry can help you learn things; it can help you see things in a different light
Some poetry is toxic to the mind
Some poetry can fill your head with new ideas or help you become a leader
Poetry is like an angel; as poetry is read, it changes people
Poetry is a good drug; it addicts people to read it
Poetry is what I love to do; I guess poetry was my calling from God

# Acquiescence
## by Dawn Killmer

You hide the truth deep inside yourself
Though you know it's wrong
Idolizing all that isn't you
All the lies have blinded you from yourself
In your mutual you are never really alone
Surrounded by all the insecure like you
Don't be afraid when the darkness fades away
And you are uncovered ... caught ... revealed
Don't try to fight ... you'll not win
Just don't be like them
The fear taking over you
The pain building up inside of you
Burns inside of me and tells me who you really are
Just listen to your heart
It will lead you back ... I promise
Don't be afraid

# Dancing Breeze
## by Kristen McIntosh

The cool swift breeze blew past me
And danced through the night sky
Swirling and tumbling softly through the palm trees
Off past the full golden moon

# I Won't Be
## by Cassity Clayton

All of my life I've worked hard for my goals
I've seen many things and touched people's souls
Right when my dreams are starting to come true
You want me to go and make love to you
But I won't be a number in some magazine
Saying, "Hey, you're a mom, are you also a teen?"
So don't even think of doing something to me
I won't give it up to you all for free
So the next time you ask what I want to do
My response will be, "Anything but you"

# Cheap Love
### by Josie Therrien and Dorothy England

A plastic flower and a greasy greeting
On what's called a romantic day
Sugar free chocolates not worth eating
In your locker they will stay
Five dollars buys the cheap dinner
Which is made with ham and cheese
This isn't worth the eye shimmer
But it does make you sneeze
With other girls he keeps on flirting
Even when you tell him how it makes you hurting
For all the months you've had to miss
He finally reaches out to kiss
Right when it's gonna happen
He says he's forgotten his chap stick
The face you used to love now needs a good slapping
Why, oh why, was he the guy you had to pick
What was once thought a happy ending
Now seems like it never was there
And maybe it was just you pretending
To be cute and to be fair


# Carmelo Anthony
### by Derek DuBois

| | |
|---|---|
| He | hour the of man The |
| Is | a |
| The | s |
| Man | got |
| Straight | the |
| Out | power, to tower any |
| Of | man |
| College | he |
| He | faces |
| Is | To |
| Here | cross- |
| To | over |
| Rule | Lebron |
| And | Anthony |
| Demolish | Jell-O like is Carmelo |

Runner Up

Liz Gildea

Now a sophomore,
Liz has invested ten years
in the Suzuki Piano Program.
She has also recently been appointed
as a member of her school's student council.
Like many of our authors, she reads constantly,
yet still finds time to participate in Girl Scouts.

# Lighter Than Air
## by Liz Gildea


I stand on the corner of two dark, diverging streets
Quietly holding a bunch of balloons
They are of many different colors
The blues just as beautiful as the reds
Some of them burst; some simply die
They fall slowly, and I watch with disappointment
Until they touch the sidewalk
But then, I sigh and smile again
And retrieve a new one from my pocket
And fill it with warm, gentle breaths
I hold on for a while
But the thin ribbon beneath my fingers isn't enough
To keep it from the inevitable breeze
Which catches me unaware
And lifts the balloon away
I couldn't bring it back if I tried
Instead, I follow with shining eyes
As it sails on its own
Toward a new sun

Victoria Adel Gibson

Victoria is in the tenth grade
and lists reading and writing as her favorite hobbies.
She is also a talented singer,
adding her voice to choirs
at both her church and school.
The sewing club and math team
round out this busy girl's extracurricular activities.

# A Birthday Wish
## by Victoria Adel Gibson


Two people sit next to each other
I asked them to and they obliged
However, I feel that if it were their way
One would not have come
But today is my day, I will not listen to fear
Today there is hope that old wounds will heal
Today I wish on twelve minute lights
That I will have to endure this separation no longer
The day was wonderful, I received many gifts
But there still was that unease of reality
And somehow I knew this was only a day
And never again would I have this union to endure
Never again will those two sit in a state of truce
Never again will they be at peace together
But today is my day, I will not listen to fear
Today I can hope that old wounds will heal
I made it my wish and I took extra care
To extinguish each light in one, giant breath
Today I wish to suffer no more
Today I dream, for upon the morrow, I wake

# Division IV
# Grades 10-12

# Commercial Glory
## by Mackenzie Sehlke

Awash in colored lights, splendid glories
Garbage decorates, sparkles divine
Billboards tell cosmopolitan stores
Streets beleaguers with refuse, waste sublime
Amid tireless toil and hectic rush
Fire burns, life is born; poet's dreams
Millions are locked in eternal crush
City survival: always more than it seems
Everyone's selling: designer suicide
Toxic smoke spews from death on a stick
Along the way, American dreams died
Breath-taking beauty, a sadistic trick
In and out we all wander, all of us lost
Blissfully unaware, progress' cost


# The Other Side
## by Elishia Appleton

Blurry, fuzzy days, I waste away; peering from behind wet glass
Normal vanished in thin air and no one cares
Blood drips out of my mouth, seeping from my eyes
What is it like to die? Can you see, can you see?
Everyone laughs as if I were a joker, merely playing a jest
My heart beats out of my chest, I evaporate into a scene above
His voice is rough, "Excuses, excuses, excuses
She's dead, you're dying, there's no sense in lying"
Sick of this, in ignorant bliss; when life slips away, light as a cloud
Only consequences and supposed suffering remain
In a world where no one can hear me
No ear sweetly hear, the blood curdling screams, the murdered dreams
Everyone in black, "Poor thing, she never had a chance"
They don't meet my glance, but I'm still here …

## Love Me Always
### by Meghan Nicole Schmidt

Love is like an ocean, very big and very deep
When I try to look down, nothing is to be seen
Love is as deep as you, farther and farther down
What is love you say?  It is an ocean
An ocean full of family, an ocean full of friends
What I like most is the love all around


## Riddle
### by Pancarte Yolene

I have many names; yet I have none
I am the emptiness, which fills the mind when all links are broken
I am the void, which sucks the body into eternal slumber
I am the shadow, which will hide the sun letting it shine upon you
I am the light, which shines in the night leaving you in the dark
I am the end; I am the beginning
All fear and hate me because I bring them peace
I am death


## Lonely
### by Lela Erickson

I sit here and wait and it seems like forever
I didn't know it would be this hard when I began this endeavor
I see only smiles and so I smile too
But inside my heart breaks because I'm thinking of you
When we're together I feel so alive
But the way I feel without you is impossible to describe
It's like living a lie because life's just not right
And without you I can't even sleep at night
I know things will change when we're together again
And when you leave I'll be lonely like I always have been

# Something Beautiful
## by Stephanie Hall

A lamb I was given to warm
From cold snows and hostile wind
Locked inside an innocent form
I had no previous errand
I was but some wool
Something beautiful
I was severed off and taken
From the only life I had known
Stretched and pulled straight I was maken'
Into a thread that brightly shown
I was but some wool
Something beautiful
Now on a spool of dark green
In pride of who I was, waited
Again taken to make a scene
The prettiest dress, untainted
I was but some wool
Something beautiful


# Big Billy
## by Shanna Carney

Billy had a big stomach, as stomachs do go
He could eat anything, even a doe!
And this is where our story began
As Billy ate a tin can
He ate the dining room mat
He then ate his father's favorite cat!
He ate a black pen
And the chair from Mom's den
He couldn't stop eating
Even after a beating
He gobbled down his house
Also his sister's pet mouse
By now he was the size of a school
And could easily drink a whole swimming pool!
Billy gulped down the city's new train
Without the slightest bit of pain
But when Billy tried to eat the town's steeple
He exploded onto all the people!

# Sorrow
### by Marlena Brown

I have sorrow at night, sorrow to fight
Maybe that's why I'm acting uptight
I hear you have someone new on your mind
So let me know now, are we a waste of time?
My love is not something that you borrow
That's why I call it sorrow
I know that I can look for better
But still, I choose you to be my forever
I know I shouldn't be bothered with you
But there's no need of lying, 'cause these feelings are true
I really want you to be all mine
Our feelings of love become intertwined
But it seems time to face the fact
Maybe you don't really love me and it's all an act
I thought what we had was love at first sight
But just to hold on to you is such a fight
I realize now that it's time to say goodbye
But just in case you're wondering why
You took my love for granted you see
And sorrow is done, it's time to do me


# Lighthouse
### by Daniel Roberts

I try my best but the world shuts me out
Chatham is a place of bumbling fools with no eyes
For everyone but me, life is easy and simple
You might ask, "How can she say that?"
But who are you to judge? You see the outside
But you haven't burnt your hand on the fiery pain that lives in me
Can I revise; can I change?
Hell with change; it's not me; it's them
I am pinned like a poster to the wall
Or am I just trapped in my head?
As I change my life does not; how can that be?
Is it me?  Or is it the changeless atmosphere
Or useless fools that surround me?
"Do I dare disturb the universe?"

# The Dreamer's Realm
## by Kaitlyn Baccoli

Gliding above the clouds, she is so eminent
Looking to the horizon, feeling the embrace of the sun
No state of mind as elusive as this; the world becomes a dreamer's realm
A captivating place of vision where only the pure of heart abide
All you see is beauty; all you feel is warmth; all you hear is silence


# As Fallen So the Fallen Rise
## by Amy Lynn Cox

The Silver Phoenix cannot rise
To soar in distant scarlet skies
As Truth in Truthless desert cries
So does the one with Twilight's Eyes
The power of Truth that can tell lies
Becomes a part of Twilight's Eyes
As Silver Phoenix glitt'ring flies
The Truthless takes a fallen prize
As Silver Phoenix falling dies
With tears in ever crimson tides
The Silver wall to Scarlet lies
But Silver Truth will always hide
As Darkness finds the Twilight's Eyes
The Silver sheen of Phoenix dies
With thorn-tied wings no Phoenix flies
As Fallen So The Fallen Rise


# Rutland Pond
## by Heather Love

Once, skating across the pond, I found a raccoon embedded in the ice
He must have ventured out too far and fallen through
Struggling first to escape, then to breathe, perhaps he pulled himself out
Lying upon the sheet of ice before falling into deep sleep
When I found him, he was stiff, limbs outstretched, beads of winter on his whiskers
In late March, the ice melted; he was visible for a few days
Before slipping beneath the cover of the pond
I don't swim there anymore

# Temporarily Yours
## by Nicole Marie Valentine Raboin Lussier

A desolate feeling
You loathe that night with ineffable death
You're waiting, trying maybe, incapable of love
Your vision of somewhere obvious, the destruction is hate
Your cry can lift a moment, hover or crash
Salty words flow, thus the reason is stuck to sudden tragedy

# Oceanic Incompetence
## by Tonka Dancikova

Over and under, around and through
Cut through my heart and eat out my soul
Abolish the gods and fight for the neurotic demons, the ones of my night
Invaluable, precious to you and those who care enough to try their hand
At impossible feats such as those which you weave
Never knowing when night will come and wake you from your sorrows
Over and under, around and through
Make up your mind and keep to the path which you have laid out
Eternal nights flowing, tentatively waiting for my sorrow to evaporate
And join you in silence, never knowing
Never ceasing to fight, to fight for eternal nights and your worthless demons

# Bring Me Down
## by Destinee Bardgett

I love you so much, do you feel it too?
I want to feel your touch; I would do anything for you
You have some problems; I have problems too
Do you love me enough to bring me down with you?
Every night as I lay down to sleep I pray to my God for your soul to keep
I want for you to be happy and to pass on while you sleep
Just so it won't cause you pain
I want to keep you up, and let you bring me down
I want to feel your love, and to keep you as my own
You say that you love me
Do you love me enough to bring me down with you?
Honey don't you see that I would do anything for you?

# Something
### by Christina Collins

Something dances in your eye
Colors grinning bold and shy
With each glance I wonder more
Have I seen that gleam before?
Something whispers in your smile
Song of some familiar isle
We have shared but just a word
Yet that voice, have I once heard?
Something tingles in your hand
Warmth I somehow understand
Though we have first met tonight
Has this palm once pressed mine tight?
Something soon gives you away
Strangely easy, when you say
"I know you, for I am sure
In my dreams we danced before"


# On the Outside
### by Kristal Shegrud

I am the sick bit of food stuck between a speaker's teeth
He doesn't know I'm there
Crowds notice me but push me from the scene
Like an incongruence, they do not stare

But there I'm wedged, unable to break free
From my false porcelain prison. How can
I live without any room left to breathe?
I'm small. How can I fight and take a stand?

I am just a bystander. I'm watching
I'm watching the world live through panes
And I'm not part of it. Yet I'm striving
Trying to find me and not leave a stain

Am I a water ring left from a cup?
I swirl. I sit. I'm left to dry up

# Dumb Farmer
## by Christopher Triplett

Once there was a farmer
Who had a mama pig and ten little piglets
The mama pig and her piglets lived in the barn among the pine trees
One day a big black cloud rolled in
The piglets became frightened and ran out into the barn yard
Mama pig ran to get them but the wind came in
It went spinning around and around
The mama pig and piglets went spinning round and around
Then the storm was over and the farmer came looking for his pigs
He couldn't find them, but he heard a noise but no pigs
Then he looked up, all his pigs hanging in a tree
"Oh my," said the farmer, "What will I do? I can't leave my pigs hanging in a tree
So he got his saw and cut the tree down
Dumb farmer


# The Gift of Life
## by Charyl Bammert

I was tired and you sat with me
I was scared and you comforted me
I was sad and you cried with me
I was happy and you laughed with me
I was down and you lifted me up
I was lost and you found me
I was cold and you held me
I was alone and you loved me
I was dead and you gave me a reason to live


# Winds Whispering Fate
## by Tyler Swank

You throw your punches like whirl wind fury
And you knock the leaves down in all their glory
When you move the clouds in
And the sky turns to the color of skin
You rip it all open letting the soft flakes fall
And the new white world surrounds us all
Then the world grows silent
And the birds know what is meant
They all fly south and in colds sublime
Like opposites of summertime

# Indigo Lies
### by Elizabeth Newton

Most people live a happy life on the surface, a simple one –
Slight pain or disappointment, but nothing we can't overcome
However, in the emerald deepness, in the dusty shadows of our eyes
There lies our mangled, broken secrets, there is kept our muffled cries
For deep blue memories are often painful
And sometimes prove too painful to escape
But with the help of understanding hands, our hope for golden healing's not too late
When sunshine's lost and hope is gone is when we all must search
Behind the crimson eyes of greying souls to look where crying spirits perch
So look behind the weary eyes of those you think you know
For behind tired eyes, dance indigo lies and hurt too deep to show


# Winner In the End
### by Angelica Porrino

You really don't have even the slightest clue
Of all the pain and hurt that I go through
I always go back to you and have no clue why
Each time it happens, all I do is cry
The time has come for it to happen once again this year
Until things are normal, I'll be full of depression and fear
Fear that things will never again be just exactly the same
But then again, I guess it's all part of your little game
All I am to you is a character for you to name and play with
But I'm a person with feelings, not some made up myth
But in your eyes, I'm still a beginner on the very first level
Guess my armor's not made of strong enough metal
You can play with my character whenever you choose
Just know that in the end you are going to lose
The time has come for me to defeat the army
I'll defeat it with a vision of you down on your knees
Down on your knees begging, "Please take me back
I made a mistake and that's a fact"
But it's all just my dream, as I wait for my turn to play
I'll be past level one, and beat this game some day!

## The Girl
### by Richelle Miller

The girl that you hold so close to your heart
With her upbeat personality and gentle nature
She wears her heart on her sleeve, but doesn't seem to care
She draws people to her yet seems naïve to what goes on around her
She wears a bright smile on her face, always laughing, always smiling
That is the girl you know and love, but do you know of her troubled heart
No, she hides her sadness with that false smile of hers
Placing her friend's happiness before her own
You claim to know this kind-hearted girl, but how much do you really know
Do you know of her pain, she hides it with a laugh, mostly keeping to herself
For she cares most about her friends and their happiness


## Down On My Luck
### by Dustin Brown

I couldn't wait to get a new car
I was going, oh, so far
Sitting in the driveway over to the side
I was looking at my very first "ride"
A Mitsubishi, shiny metallic gray
I vowed my car would stay that way
Driving around town, cruising at night
I didn't realize my future plight
Then one day my luck went bad
I experienced the worst I've ever had
They told me first it was the computer box
And didn't know how much it would cost
Next went the timing chain
What's that quote about the rain?
Oh yeah, when it rains it pours
My car is locked behind garage doors
This is the worst luck I've ever had
Thinking about it makes me mad
No one should have this kind of luck
Next time, I think I'll buy a truck

# If Wishes Were Fishes
## by Megan Kittridge

If I could only write a poem
I would write one about you and the glimpse of beauty I saw
Flash for an instant in those deep brown eyes
Before it sprinted off like a frightened deer back to the forest
I would capture that moment and hold it close
Then gently set it down on paper as to not wrinkle it
Then I would let the world see what is behind your eyes
A feeling so great it must be shared
Oh, if I could only write a poem


# My Struggle
## by Guy Pistone

The O is the infinity of my thoughts
C is for the craziness of the actions I cannot stop
D gives disability, death to one's mind; this is what my head is like all the time
Trust me this will be over in an hour, 3 hours later I am at the same spot
Like the constant drip of water in the shower
Every action or thought turns into a waste of time
My head is the Vietnam War and prison combined
I am waiting to get out of this tunnel without a light
I just fall as a string does without its kite
I try so hard to hide, to stop the world from seeing this demon built up inside
But with arms wide it embraces me with love
I know it kills me but it is a soothing drug
No it is not, it is like 100 crawling bugs
I am wrong, it is a beautiful highflying dove
Do not say that, it's a body covered in blood
But every time I end up giving in, it gives me a hug
But in the end I know it takes my mind and fills it with floods
Stop pushing me so hard; no, please, I can't do another minute
I already did it 500 times; I got to quit it
But it pushes me harder, like a drill sergeant to his soldiers
It's like a boulder on my shoulders stopping me from moving forwards
This is over now, it's a wrap
But I can feel it coming on again; a cobra always bites back

# Alone
### by Amanda Alexander

Sitting here all alone, wanting you here
My face is wet and my long hair is down
Why did you leave me? Were you full of fear?
Your face is stained with a lingering frown
No smile appears, not one sees the day
You lit up my life for less than a year
I found you cold in the flowers of May
I thought I could warm you, chase away fear
You ran, did you have no love for me?
We laughed and played; it was all just a game
I chose to be blind; I chose not to see
I am to blame, what a feeling of shame
Without you here, my life has no more pain
Without you here, I may finally gain


# The Lost Lamb
### by Ryan Wilson

I am just a lamb, who chose not to listen to Your orders
Now my heart aches; the pain is unbearable
I thought I could find greener pastures
But all I found was dead grass, thorns, and sadness
That valley that was promised by them was not green
Why did I stray away from You?
I should have stayed within Your fields of milk and honey, yet I did not
Curiosity drowned out my conscience and lured me to search elsewhere
The sin I committed was merely caused by human nature
Now, I ask of Your forgiveness, to remove the blood from my wound
To purify me with Your blessed everlasting waters of love
I wish to become a faithful servant of Yours
To put behind my flaws and begin anew
To dedicate my life to You and entrust absolute faith
That shall be placed into Your glorious hands
By You guiding me, Lord, I know my life will be of love
Sometimes, I may even question but I should always trust You
Please guide this lost lamb of Yours
This lamb that is me

# Our Last Car Crash
## by Patrick Wynne

Nothing's clear when fog tints those windshield eyes
And your glass tears are too sharp to grace this cheek
But just in case, here's my hand to wipe away those pieces
The pieces that once built up a mirror image of what could be
So what's it going to be?
Will we slow down, or speed up?
Death by highway's never been so beautiful as it is with you
So take my hand in yours and breathe in deep
Let's see who holds on longest
I promise I won't let go


# Someone
## by Miranda MacMillan

There is always someone worse off than you
I wish you would understand, I wish you knew
Something is always wrong, nothing is ever right
Some people don't even have anyone to tuck them in at night
They don't know I love you's, they don't know friends
They don't know what life is, until it ends
Some don't have parents; some have no one at all
At least you have one person to call
Someone to call a friend, someone who cares
Someone who wants to let you know, that they will always be there


# A Tear Ever So Shed
## by Faith Wanja

I shed a tear, so lonely a tear
Yet so solemnly intact my tear remains
So loud and hard a yelling it tells
Of perpetual pain and anger and hurt
A yearning, a scream of distort
You name it, it claims it
This ... a tear, so lonely a tear
How small it is, so much it holds
Its strength and power so hard to comply
Strong! It so ever stands
Its image that never hands!
Do you see this tear?
Oh, so lonely a tear?

# Exhaustion
## by Jennie Guido

Exhaustion
Filling every fiber of my being
Eternity
The length of my never-ending day
Fight
Trying to go on for just one more minute
Heavy
Every second is another weight added to my drooping shoulders
Sleep
Finally overtakes me
And as my head hits the pillow ... dreams


# The Sunrise
## by Benjamin Picillo

Oh, there beneath the sullen break of day
There lurks the truth that haunts the mind of man!
To hide the key is nature's twisted way
Of tempting souls to live the veil of plan
That twists and pulls the heart to beat
In constant rhythm of the wind-whipped land
The sun does lack the light to call defeat
But there, while rays do move in desire
He may attempt to see what is discrete
There is no way to find what transpired
Yet there, while rays do move in reverence
The knowledge of the seeped sun conspires
He learns to leave the holy temperance
Of day's rebirth: the dreaded severance


# A Glass of Water
## by Marie Rivers

I was once an ocean, a lake, a river
Always flowing and tumbling
I was once blue as the sky and white as the waves
Multifaceted with every color gazing from my depths
But now I am trapped, stagnant as if time has stopped
Reduced to a single shade of clear
You can change what I look like, not who I am
But for now, I am just a glass of water

## Only Yourself
### by Matt Ibrahim

This soliloquy I speak
Is killing me, it's deep
Because it shatters my voice
And inside, I feel weak
I know I'm the only one who feels the way I do
But I keep to myself, because it doesn't mean a thing to you
I took a second to think and my thoughts came to me
Because no one truly cares for another, as far I can see
I may be blind, but I can see the truth
I can see it deep within you
And trust is something I hold true
Because it's frustrating
Having people lie to your face
My trust's aching
And it's sad to see them go about their ways
As if what they're doing isn't wrong
To know that they've been two-faced all along
It's a pity, but it only makes you strong
To put up with it and carry on
As an individual, because they're all gone


## Growin' Up
### by Ryan Weaver

Watching Power Rangers on TV
Eating Spaghetti-O's on the kitchen counter
Playing in the ditch behind the house
Building tree houses in the woods
Skating all over downtown
Running from Securitas and Wackenhuts
Eating at Keifer's Greek restaurant
Skipping the check when we were finished
Going to parties in my new car
Staying out real late
Going to work in the mornings
Wakeboarding in the afternoons

# Fly For Fish
## by Justin Sarette

An eagle flies to hunt
Eagle swoops stealthily over
Silent river of fish
Splashing sharp talons
Floating off with a fish

# Chocolate
## by Matthew Litchfield

Chocolate, a sweet royalty with a divine crunch
Something you don't want to eat during brunch
The milky taste
That you eat with much haste
The decorations in which they are covered
Makes you think just what you've discovered

# When the Lights Go Down
## by Arynne Noel Belger

All alone when the lights go down
A dazed dream sweeps my mind
All the years of sweat, blood, and tears
Vanishes into the past behind
No one watching, I light up the stage
My deepest desires take me away
To the place I long to be
Sweet memories call and warm my heart
The stage calls me near
Yearning to be in the spotlight
In the heat of the moment my senses delight
Through the make up and smiles try to hide
How it feels to be quivering inside
Someday, I will be the prima ballerina in the main stream
Nevertheless, for now, I'm all alone
When the lights go down

# From Above
## by Kate Scheffey

Above all life
I gaze down to Earth
And I see the squares
That hold our land
From here we look peaceful
And almost serene
The wispy clouds
Drift across the glass
Shading my view of the ground
I begin to wonder what it's like
In far off places
The mystery and adventure
Of a foreign land


# Climbing the Ladder To Success
## by Shanarne Williams

I am climbing the ladder to success and I will take it one step at a time
I will make it all the way to the top and success will definitely be mine
The first step will surely get me started then I will be on my determined way
Going to school, striving to be the best, and studying hard each and every day
Climbing the ladder will not be easy and this I definitely already know
To find success, this is the way to go
I will need encouragement, motivation, and perseverance through and through
Along with my loving parents and teachers, success will inevitably be in view


# I Can Only Imagine
## by Stefani Stockinger

I can only imagine how it would have been
To have been born into the world back then
To have gone through all the things that Jesus did
So that we may live
His life, His death, and His love
Will always be
So that we may see all the things He did for us
So that we may be with Him for eternity

# Captured
## by Annemarie Herzing

I once was free from my enemy
But somehow they captured me
My head beats with pain
I feel all the blame
There is nowhere to hide
And no one there by my side
My tears start to fall
They create a river that searches for the sea
My sky is no longer blue; it is dark and weary
It is very scary
Surrounded by feelings I fear
I am lost and cold with no one near
I should have never told; should I run towards the light
I'm not sure ... is that right?


# If Only
## by Christina Miller

There's a girl with a broken smile
It may heal after a while
Right now she doesn't have a single best friend
Only God is there to guide her to the end
She feels like she's been played with like a toy
Her heart cannot be broken by another boy
Sure, he said he loved her and then took his life
But they were so young, unlikely to become man and wife
Why do some things end so tragic?
If only they'd used some common sense, some logic
A life is something that cannot be replaced
People miss such a sweet embrace
Everything turns suddenly all too still
You want it to go away but it never will
Life happens and life goes away
Many wish you'd made the choice to stay
It came so sudden I couldn't believe
But my only feelings now are of grief
I know you didn't mean to cause so much despair
If only you'd known how much we all still care

Adam Valdez

Presently in the eleventh grade,
Adam is an active member in his school's
chess club and philosophy club.
Musically inclined,
he lists the guitar as his favorite instrument,
and has been taking lessons for the past year.

Tranquility & Chaos
by Adam Valdez


Tranquility, that four-syllable sound
With so much bliss
Tranquility is peppermint breath
Blue skies, cooing birds, and the toss of a woman's hair
I live for the peace of mind
Yet, I'm ashamed to say, Chaos seems more pleasing
Lust, Greed, and Entropy, all wonderful things!
The crashing of plates, the smog filled skies
The taste of alcohol on the lips, how delightfully delicious
Tranquility and Chaos my two favorite girlfriends
I'm just glad that they'll never be in the same room together ...

Sara Marie Johnson

Now in the eleventh grade, Sara is a passionate writer.
Whether it's in her creative writing class at school,
or between readings at a local bookstore,
she seizes every opportunity to develop her talent,
putting special emphasis on poetry.
Sara's passion has not only earned Division Honors,
but also this year's Editor's Choice Award.
Congratulations Sara!

It gives us great pleasure to present
Sara Marie Johnson's
award winning poem entitled, "Father"

Father
by Sara Marie Johnson


A four-year-old princess
Stood on a folding chair
The painted smile on her face
Was pure and innocent
She was blinded by the pink flowers
That decorated her dress
And the cheap smiles her dad
Gave to the stranger across the room
The smell of his cologne
And Captain Morgan's rum
That still lingered on his breath
Made her nauseous
Chills ran up her spine
And she squirmed
While his fingers circled her back
His nostrils were coated
With powdered sugar
That gave him the energy
To be her knight and shining father

# Index of Authors

## A

Abdallah, Jacqueline  58
Agudelo, Eliana  55
Aguirre, Thomas  168
Airey, Julia Beth  19
Albers, Whitney  47
Albulet, Jenna  38
Alexander, Amanda  207
Alleyne, Lexis  161
Almeida, Ashley A.  109
Alvarez, Omar A., Jr.  70
Amero, Julia  91
Amor, Ian  177
Anderson, Ben  103
Anglesey, Marianne  152
Appleton, Elishia  196
Arenas, Kayla-Marie  23
Arthur, Cassandra  88
Audet, Brandon  48
Ayala, Justin  56

## B

Babroudi, Seda  98
Baccoli, Kaitlyn  200
Bacon, Chelsea  123
Bailey, Sikia  161
Baker, Josh  93
Balasco, John  48
Baldo, Ashley  151
Bammert, Charyl  203

Barcelos, Michael D.  97
Barden, Leslie  55
Bardgett, Destinee  201
Barnett, Matthew  122
Bartlett, Zachary  160
Bean, Victoria Ruth  81
Beatty, Sarah  59
Beauregard, Christopher  150
Becker, Scott  43
Beckstrand, Chase W.  139
Belanger, Bethany  42
Belger, Arynne Noel  211
Bembenek, Tyler  107
Bennett, Lauren A.  10
Benoit, Chené  72
Benotti, Erin  78
Berryman, Autumn  65
Bessasparis, Stephen  110
Beville, Ashley  58
Bigelow, Amber  86
Bilbo-Gildersleeve, Peri  13
Bishop, Christopher Lee  64
Bishop, Matthew S.  140
Blackman, Madeleine  12
Bolotin, Chad  11
Bolshaw, Ben  111
Bolster, Brandon  14
Borges, Rainie  10
Bousquet, Katie  81
Bowers, Kelsea Millie  68

Boylan, Molly  39
Breen, Patricia  46
Brewster, Stephanie  17
Brinkley, A.J.  103
Brockman, Jessica  110
Brogdon, Jennifer  186
Brown, Cody  144
Brown, Dustin  205
Brown, Elizabeth  156
Brown, K. Matthew  51
Brown, Mahlik  65
Brown, Marlena  199
Brown, Molly  105
Brown, Sam  179
Buer, Sarah  122
Buffington, Rebecca  112
Bugbee, Cameron  23
Bullington, Ashley  146
Burgess, Kylie  142
Burnett, Ilena  32
Butterfield, Chantel  121
Butterworth, Joshua C.  169
Byrne, Jennifer Lynn  29

## C

Cafferty, Tyler  111
Caldwell, Paris  37
Campbell, Ben  83
Campbell, Domonique  23
Caprile, Lauren  37
Carley, Ross  94

# Index of Authors

Carlson, James 184
Carney, Shanna 198
Casey, Laura Christine 18
Casey, Samantha 164
Chadbourne, Mark 161
Chaney, Alex 104
Childers, Kaitlynn 118
Cipollone, Matthew 179
Cirillo, Casey 40
Clarkson, Emma 66
Clayton, Cassity 188
Cluff, Chelsea 98
Cobar, Gabriella 13
Cokotis, Julie 46
Cole, Grace 36
Collins, Christina 202
Conlon, Tori 175
Connell, Tyler 71
Conti, Nicole 176
Corcoran, Theresa 54
Cormier, Brittany 74
Cornavaca, Ellida 90
Costa, Katelyn 115
Courtney, Jason 121
Cova, Erica 108
Cox, Amy Lynn 200
Criswell, Kayla 22
Crowley, Megan 101
Cummings, Miranda 24
Curtis, Janay N. 149
Curtis, Kaylie 45

## D

Dame, Dani 37
Dancikova, Tonka 201
Davis, Caitlin 164
Davis, Kelsey E. 178
Davis, Ty'Ara 85
Delaney, Ryan 50
Dellisola, Matt 53
Dillard, Tiffany Jade 160
Dionne, Meghan 90
Divine, Brandy 38
Doherty, Kathleen 174
Donellan, Kate 107

Dourado, Filipe 93
DuBois, Derek 189
Duda, Heather 51
Dudley, Lora 128
DuLong, Casey 98
Dupuy, Kiara 102
Durosier, Nadine 130

## E

Eacrett, Allison 10
East, Nadia 50
Ekengren, Adam 29
Eklund, Brittney 118
Elliott, Lindsey Kaye 167
England, Dorothy 189
Enyeart, Kelli 181
Erickson, Lela 197

## F

Fink, Ryan 60
Finkbeiner, James 120
Fiorello, Ariana 57
Fitts, Christina 96
Fitzpatrick, Jessica 14
Flynn, Emily 119
Flynn, Kaitlyn 36
Foley, Brynn 31
Fortier, Josh 25
Franco, Megan 122
Franke, William Reid 166
Franklin, Jasmyn 91
Fridley, Colt 153

## G

Gallagher, Connor H. 80
Garrett, Alexis 87
Gaziano, Michael 32
Gebo, Katelynn 44
Gerard, Alex 44
Gerges, Sarah 115
Gestl, Cassie 16
Giakoumis, Michael 44
Gibson, Sarah 138
Gibson, Victoria Adel 192

Gildea, Liz 190
Gilligan, Rebecca 31
Godfrey, Kelsie 21
Goff, Jerrick 151
Goodson, Ashley 123
Goodwin, Felicia 89
Graham, Emily 134
Grant, Monika 25
Grayton, Christine 85
Griffin, Nicholas 41
Grimes, Christy 120
Grit, Carly 47
Gross, Dennis, Jr. 142
Grzywna, Ali 167
Guido, Jennie 209
Gunn, Caleb 127
Guzman, Melinda G. 15

## H

Hall, Katherine 11
Hall, Stephanie 198
Hamlett, Elizabeth 123
Hammond, Byron 126
Hamrick, Lauren 95
Happnie, Kaitlin P. 172
Harding, Chelsea 88
Harding, Lauren T. 12
Harrington, Josh 25
Harris, Angelique 124
Hartle, Nicholas 48
Hassan, Alisha 125
Hebert, Andrew 63
Heggen, Tonnie 44
Heins, Phoebe 28
Hellums, Elena C. 65
Henderson, Terri 187
Hennigar, Avery 124
Hennington, Blair 80
Henry, Alexis 162
Henry, Zelika 97
Herzberg, Loucinda 114
Hicks, McKenzie 183
Hill, Linda Lorraine 148
Hillyard, Austin 61
Hoffman, Jenna 89

# Index of Authors

Holliday, Jacey 129
Holloway, Arica 69
Holmes, Danee' 130
Howe, Mitchel 153
Hoxhalli, Erisa 40
Huggins, Francina 185
Hutner, Kimberly 34

## I

Ibrahim, Matt 210
Irving, Breanna L. 127

## J

Jackson, Sean 143
James, Andrea 100
Jaqua, Lauren 104
Jelley, David 140
Jenkins, Robert S. 15
Johnson, Daniel 12
Johnson, Lacresha J. 114
Johnson, Sara Marie 216
Johnson, Tia Kamil 54
Johnston, Charly 185
Jolly, Blake 177
Jones, Alex 173
Joyce, Kara 54
Judd, Amanda 67
Judge, Deirdre 165

## K

Karistianos, Jennifer 159
Keen, Rachel 20
Keilig, Pamela 172
Kemp, Talia 168
Kenner, Daniel 110
Kester, Katherine P. 49
Kilcoyne, Mary 106
Killmer, Dawn 188
Kim, Min 153
King, Hannah 29
Kittridge, Megan 206
Korsko, Giovanni 38
Kossick, Courtney 32
Kurpiel, Allison 27
Kusmirek, Katryna 27

## L

LaFerriere, Nic 117
Lafferty, Candace 96
LaJeunesse, Cally Anne 53
Lam, Kevin 155
Lamarre, Tanisha Rose 119
Lamisere, Dimitri 109
Landeen, Kevin 148
Lavoie, Nathalie 56
Leblanc, Kristopher 67
Leiterman, Andy 154
Lenny, Traci J. 174
Lewis, Kourtney 95
Lindsay, Kameko 116
Litchfield, Matthew 211
Littell, Mason 158
Lizama, Alexzandra Eve 84
Long, Stephen 81
Love, Heather 200
Lovett, Kortney 63
Lowery, Breonna 128
Luchs, Abigail 33
Luchs, Tom 157
Lussier, Nicole 201

## M

MacMillan, Miranda 208
Mahler, Haley 99
Mahmoud, Nadia 173
Maier, Maria 62
Mali, Tulsi 42
Man, Jacky 103
Mann, Elliott 27
Manton, April 149
Maples, Cortney 163
Margulis, Kate 92
Martin, Josh 80
Martin, Kelly 16
Martin, Mary Lou 94
Mason, Taylor 41
Mathews, Dustin C. 65
Mazurowski, Dana 61
McCammon, Paxton 55
McCann, Bailey 132

McCarthy, Tess 33
McCune, James William 162
McHaney, Megan 52
McIntosh, Kristen 188
McKenzie, Hannah-Grace 31
Meads, Marianne 185
Medovich, Corey 92
Medrano, Matthew 42
Memme, Sabrina 144
Miera, Nicholas P. 126
Miller, Richelle 205
Minahan, Matthew 158
Mitchell, Christina 91
Mixon, Leia 120
Mofford, Mindy 112
Mondry, Andrew Paul 152
Moore, Brady 147
Moran, Tommy 33
Moriarty, Josh 178
Morris, Jessica Marie 116
Morrocco, Casey 157
Moulton, Andrew 181
Murphy, Keyonna 26
Myrtil, Leah Victoria 26

## N

Nash, Takashi 34
Nassoura, David 82
Neisess, Margaret 87
Nettleship, Molly 112
Neu, Laura 172
Newton, Elizabeth 204
Nguyen, Teresa 101
Nishimiya, Akiyo 94
Novoa, Nandinii 176
Nunez, Anaissa 71

## O

O'Callaghan, Stasha 82
Ochoa, Enrique 41
O'Connor, Mallory 180
Oderman, Alexandra 141
Olsen, Kristin 151
O'Neil, Danielle 169
Ordog, Norbert 105

# *Index of Authors*

Orr, Danielle 35
Ortega, Alexis 66
O'Shea, Kelsey 171
Oswald, Ashlee 45
O'Toole, Diana E. 41
Owens, Samantha 58

**P**

Pacheco, Barbara 108
Paré, Alexandria 146
Patrick, Amber 30
Payne, Ariana Lynn 84
Payne, Chanta 59
Pelletier, Brooke 39
Pelletier, Jessica 52
Pelletier, Talia 113
Penndorf, Taylor C. 26
Petersen, Jada 66
Petersen, Kati 145
Petri, Christian 17
Pham, Loan 78
Picillo, Benjamin 209
Pierce, Kyler 99
Pistone, Guy 206
Pitchios, Cody 57
Pitts, Bryonna 128
Pitts, Victoria M. 82
Polderman, Laurie 182
Porrino, Angelica 204
Porterfield, Jori 18
Poulos, Sophia 39
Pruitt, Savanah 27

**Q**

Quinn, Samantha 64

**R**

Rabinowitz, Moshe 104
Rapoport, Luiza 179
Rathjen, Sydney 29
Rausch, Corrin 171
Ray, Kellen 106
Reed, Kevin 96
Regan, Catherine 14
Remling, Logan 64

Repetti, Katlin 40
Rhodes, Nicholas 42
Rhodes, Taylor 69
Rhodes, Tori 18
Rice, Megan 160
Rios, Amanda V. 24
Risica, Daniel 145
Rivers, Marie 209
Rizley, Karlie 156
Robb, David 169
Robb, Katie 117
Roberts, Daniel 199
Roberts, Sarah 53
Roberts, Scott 116
Robinson, Devin 125
Robinson, Stephanie 154
Rodriguez, Alexis 59
Rodriguez, Brandon J. 15
Rogers, Amanda E. 113
Roser, Madelon 52
Rothchild, Leah 83
Rotz, Zachary 165
Rowland, Casey 36
Rowlett, Marissa K. 20
Rush, Sean 85
Russell, Samantha 79
Russo, Emily 78
Russo, Madeline 34

**S**

Sacra, Craig 170
Sanford, Alexandra 28
Sanford, Suzanne 43
Sarette, Justin 211
Sarle, Cody 148
Saunders, Lee 129
Scheffey, Kate 212
Scheffey, Lillie 150
Schmidt, Meghan N. 197
Schultz, Stevie 17
Sehlke, Mackenzie 196
Sellers, Brooklyn 111
Sellers, Jocelyn 162
Sentilles, Jessica 180
Serrazina, Vincent 168
Shaevel, Louis B. 50

Sharp, Sarah 175
Shegrud, Kristal 202
Simon, Lyndsay 166
Sipos, Timea 10
Skelly, Kendall 138
Slemmer, Tiffany 106
Smith, Cory 113
Smith, Erin 117
Smith, Karisa Lyn 174
Smith, Meghan 68
Sportsman, Kapua 59
Springer, Emma 159
St. Paul, Jade 58
St.Pierre, Torieana A. 22
Staley, Alyssa 105
Stark, Lauren 24
Starzecki, Spencer 103
States, Broderick R. 20
Sterba, Amber 129
Steward, Casey 50
Stratton, Jessica 68
Sun, Alice 19
Svedin, Audrey 66
Svedin, Jolene 47
Swan, Ashley 158
Swank, Tyler 203
Swenson, Jocelyn 16
Sylvia, Althea 79

**T**

Talbot, Tailor 109
Tang, Kevin 49
Tapp, Maxx 118
Taylor, Ashley N. 170
Taylor, Daja 35
Tedemet, Tadela 57
Tenggren, Kasey 51
Theodosiou, Alejandro 94
Therrien, Josie 189
Thompson, Nina 92
Tidwell, Lacie 178
Tougias, Brian 173
Tracy, Maia 40
Triplett, Christopher 203
Tucker, Kasie 60
Tur, Peri 13

# Index of Authors

## U

Ulmer, Andy 167
Unruh, Mason M. 21
Urban, Karen 181

## V

Valdez, Adam 214
Valvero, Berkley E. 121
van Mulbregt, Emily 43
Vargas, Shannon 35
Vinson, Julia 184
Vogt, Taylor 30

## W

Wagner, Kathryne 186
Walker, Wendy 147
Wanja, Faith 208
Wasti, Faisal Rashid 63
Watkins, Shelby 131
Weatherly, Tucker 176
Weaver, Ryan 210
Webb, Bryan 100
Wegner, Josy 141
Weisman, Taylor 21
Weiss, Jocelin 99
Wells, Daniel 56
White, Krista 102
Wiech, Christina 166
Williams, Colin 34

Williams, Darrien 46
Williams, Shanarne 212
Wilson, Erica N. 155
Wilson, Ryan 207
Winters, Dustin 67
Winzeler, Alexandra 143
Woodbridge, Sarah 123
Woods, Shyanna 22
Word, Alisa 15
Worley, Nicholas 163
Wortz, Alyssa 45
Wright, Ashly 183
Wright, Korena 102
Wu, Lisa 19
Wynne, Patrick 208

## Y

Yolene, Pancarte 197
Yordy, Nicholas 95

## Z

Zamora, Valerie 152
Zatir, Sara J. 146
Zeger, Maxine 125
Zele, Damon 48
Zemanek, Rachael Hannah 28
Zimmerman, Jacy 184
Zink, Shayna 139
Zizza, J.R., Jr. 30

# *Gifted*
## *Price List*

Initial Copy...................................32.95

Additional Copies............................ 24.00

*Please Enclose $6  Shipping/Handling Each Order

Check or Money Order Payable to:

The America Library of Poetry
P.O. Box 978
Houlton, Maine 04730

Must specify book title and author

Please Allow 21 Days For Delivery

THE AMERICA
LIBRARY OF POETRY

www.libraryofpoetry.com
Email: generalinquiries@libraryofpoetry.com

# Poetry On the Web

## See Your Poetry Online!

This is a special honor reserved exclusively for our published poets.

Now that your work has been forever set in print,
why not share it with the world at www.libraryofpoetry.com

At the America Library of Poetry,
our goal is to showcase quality writing in such a way as to inspire
others to broaden their literary horizons,
and we can think of no better way to reach people around the world
than by featuring poetic offerings like yours on our global website.

Since we already have your poem in its published format,
all you need to do is copy the information from the form below on
a separate sheet of paper, and return it with a $6 posting fee.
This will allow us to display your poetry
on the internet for one full year.

Author's Name _____

Poem Title _____

Book Title _____ *Gifted* _____

Mailing Address _____

City_____ State_____ Zip Code _____

Check or Money Order in the amount of $6 payable to:
The America Library of Poetry
P.O. Box 978
Houlton, Maine 04730